College Ruined Our Daughter

College Ruined Our Daughter

Letters to Parents Concerning the
Baffling World of the College Student

by Wesley Shrader

1817

HARPER & ROW, PUBLISHERS

New York, Evanston, and London

LIBRARY OF CONGRESS CATALOG CARD NUMBER: 69-17010

To
Betsy
Ellen
Scott
Kelly
—my joyful involvement with a new generation

Contents

Preface

This book deals with the personal alienation between adults, particularly parents, and the young people of this generation. Characters are introduced, situations analyzed, problems presented, and specific suggestions are sometimes offered. However, the reader will find little preaching and virtually no moralizing. "College Ruined Our Daughter" attempts to describe the reasons for the anger, confusion, and bewilderment of parents; it is also an attempt to offer some explanation of "how our young people got that way" as well as their response to the pressures upon them. Above all, it is a plea for understanding and acceptance by those who live and love in the two worlds of those over thirty and those under thirty.

In recent years I have visited a number of countries outside of the United States, including England, France, Holland, Germany the Scandinavian countries, Poland, and the Soviet Union. In these countries I had contact with both adults and college-age young people. It is my experience that the alienation between parents and children in the United States is characteristic of every country I visited, including Poland and the Soviet Union. It may be the phenomenon of our time.

There are those who will say that today's young people do not want to participate creatively in the structures of our society, that they are intent on "overthrowing the government" and "destroying the free-enterprise system." I say this is nonsense and that such irresponsible charges will get us nowhere as we try to solve the problems immediately ahead. The great mass of young people have no intention of overthrowing the government, nor do they wish to abolish the free-enterprise system. They only want to make the government strong where it has been weak, to make it effective where it has been ineffective, and to make "free enterprise" work in those areas where it has dismally failed. They will not wait until college graduation or after graduate school to "do their thing"—they want "in" now.

These young people, who are demanding a piece of the action, are not only pressing for a more just social order, they, like their European contemporaries, are challenging two venerable institutions in our national life. These are, first, the traditional forms of religion as expressed by today's institutional church and second, the traditional patterns of love, sex and marriage. Those of the "older" generation may look with horror upon these challenges but that they exist in power few will deny.

The author of this book neither criticizes nor condones the responsible thrusts for change in these, our most cherished institutions. He is convinced, however, that changes are taking place and will continue to do so. Thus it is his hope that some of these changes can pave the way for improvement upon society as we have known it in the past.

WESLEY SHRADER

Lewisburg, Pennsylvania

I
To Mr. Grabowski,
concerning his son Ed

Mr. All-American

Dear Mr. Grabowski,

Let me first of all congratulate you on being elected president of the New York Kingston Alumni Club. You have always been a strong supporter of the college, especially in the field of athletics. I know the administration appreciates your efforts.

It was a pleasure for my wife and me to be your guests at the last home game. Apparently Ed made all the arrangements. He wanted me to meet his father; he's very proud of you. In this day when we see so much of family estrangement, it is an inspiration to know of the bond between you and your son.

At any rate, victory was sweet, Ed made the winning touchdown, the wine was delicious, the dinner superb. I also want to thank you for the nice things you said about Helen. I agree she's a doll—and I'm not going to trade her in!

Things must have been tough for you when you were a student at Kingston. You said that your football scholarship saved your life, that you could not have made it without direct aid for your athletic prowess. As we read the records today, we see nothing of your struggle to remain in school, only the story of Al Grabowski, "candidate for All-American honors"—the best running back in Kingston's history.

That is, the best till Ed. As you no doubt know, your son has already broken all your records, including touchdown passes, and I know this must fill you with pride rather than any kind of jealousy. He is a great fellow in every sense of the word. Admired by his teammates, respected by the faculty, and adored by the fans. It is enough to turn a young man's head. But he's modest and unassuming and hardly knows that at the moment he is Kingston's greatest claim to fame—a real celebrity.

I must also mention that in addition to being adored by

Kingston fans, he is a hero to all the underprivileged children
in the city. Every Sunday afternoon he meets with a group of
Negro boys in a character-building program. He also instructs
them in weight-lifting. They love it.

I write to say that the rumor was true. Pro scouts from the
Giants, Packers, and Eagles have been in the stands throughout
the season. They are not waiting for his senior year. They want
to see him in action as a junior, and they are seeing plenty, as
last Saturday indicated. Of course, they cannot sign him until
he finishes his senior year. I don't want to appear mercenary,
but whoever signs Ed should pay through the nose, a real
Namath price tag. There are three more games to go this season, the big one this Saturday. I hope you can make it back
for one of them. If you can, give me a ring and we'll go out on
the town again.

Perhaps we could also invite Professor Hazel Spires, who
teaches political science. Her husband died about three years
ago, no children. I feel reasonably sure she would go with us to
the game (though she is no football fan) and to a supper club
afterward. Mrs. Spires is high on Ed and appears to have had
quite an influence on his thinking. She is not very impressed
with his football prowess, but says he is her best student in
"Urban Crisis in the United States." She claims his insights,
analysis, and suggestions are mature beyond his years.

Ed comes by my office quite often and we just sit and chat.
It makes me feel good to know that he is comfortable around a
chaplain (who is past thirty). Many students will not give me
the time of day. He talks a great deal about you and obviously
has respect for you, not simply because you made it big at Kingston, but because from nowhere you have gone to the top in
the garment business. He feels close to you also because, since
Mrs. Grabowski's death, you have been both father and mother

to him. He often talks about his mother and the financial struggle you had in the early years.

When he speaks of you, he laughs and says you gave him a football at age three, you taught him how to run, kick, and pass; you never missed one of his high-school games, and you knew exactly what to say when the team won and when it lost.

In recent weeks Ed has been reflective; not moody exactly, but reflective. He has posed some pointed queries concerning my job as a minister. What kind of education is needed, types of courses in a theological school, and the penetrating question: how do I live with the preacher image?

He knows I am an all-out football fan, but with me he never discusses football or anything to do with athletics. He appears obsessed by the problems of the day: the ravages of poverty in a nation of affluence, of starvation in a nation which must hoard its grain and grant money to farmers for not growing corn, cows, and pigs; of the life in the ghetto, discrimination in jobs, housing, etc. Of course, I shall follow these concerns of Ed with considerable interest, and if there are any developments I'll let you know.

Sincerely yours,
W. S.

The Poison of Hypocrisy

DEAR MR. GRABOWSKI,

I am stunned.

All I can say is, I am stunned. Kingston is stunned, the alumni are stunned, the administration is stunned, and I know that you are not only stunned, but your disappointment must continue to be difficult to bear.

As I get the story, Ed went to head coach Baker and made his announcement. He was turning in his uniform; he would never again play football, college or professional. Ed told Coach Baker that he thought he was the finest coach in the business and that it had been a pleasure playing for him. He appreciated the courteous way the coach treated him and the other players, he said, and there was nothing personal in his decision. But he was through—finished—he would never play football again.

Baker was struck as if by a sledge hammer. The game with Dartmouth is next Saturday. Why? Ed said it was a little hard to explain. Playing intercollegiate football had become a charade, and he despises it. Professional football is more honest, but that too is a joke, a sad way to spend one's life. He wanted "out" and he wanted it now. Baker's response was typical and understandable: "You can't do this to me!"

The next evening, after turning in his uniform, Ed came by my house and we had a long discussion. During the conversation he was bitter only once and that was when he spoke of the three myths surrounding football. These are: a. *Football teaches you sportsmanship.* If stepping in the face of an opponent is sportsmanship, and if attempting to break the leg of a teammate in order to start as a varsity player in next Saturday's game is sportsmanship, words have lost their meaning. b. *It is not to win or lose but how you play the game that matters.* No player in intercollegiate or professional football believes this nonsense. It remains for the coaches to reject the statement outright. Their precarious jobs demand that such a sentiment be considered trash. Coaches have little difficulty in communicating how they feel about this to their players. c. *Football prepares you for the game of life.* This is an insult to life. Football is beef, brawn, and strategy. It is played with the intent of outwitting the other man completely or doing him as much physical damage as possible. Players who take football seriously make the mistake of believing it has really "prepared them for life." But Ed wanted to know how many personal, national, or international problems are ever solved by brute strength and mere strategy? This use of force may be what is wrong with the world: might does not make right, no matter how adroitly used. In most instances, beef and military strategy are poor substitutes for economic and diplomatic power. The bull or bear can wreck a china shop, but it can also bring down the censure of world opinion on the head of a jet-happy, tank-happy nation.

Ed's decision was not taken on the spur of the moment; he had been thinking about it ever since high school. He replayed for me the last game of his high-school career. His team was unbeaten and picked to win by several touchdowns. As you undoubtedly remember, the team lost by one point, and it lost because Ed dropped an easy pass in the end zone with fifteen seconds to play. Students who earlier had carried him on their shoulders derided him—several of the players on the team called him "chicken," and the coach refused to speak to him for the rest of the school year. This was the beginning of his disenchantment with the great sport of football. He kept it to himself. At Kingston he has ridden the crest of a popularity unparalleled in the school's history. The players would die for him, the student body loves him, and Stew Baker respects every inch of him.

Then what has happened? The young widow, Professor Spires, has had a strong influence on him. She has convinced him that the game of intercollegiate football is a racket, that it is empty and meaningless. Instead of beating his brains out every day in practice and at the game on Saturday, she feels Ed should be investing his time in activities that would mean something to people—now, and not after he graduates. And she has made him feel it.

She further insists that the entire structure of college football is shot through with hypocrisy, so that whoever plays must share in the hypocrisy until he becomes as cynical as the adults who direct it and keep it alive. There are rules governing the recruitment of high-school players. Everybody knows they are flagrantly violated, if not totally ignored. Football scholarships and grants are supposed to be limited. But a local businessman had quietly announced that next week Ed would have a handsome sports car at his disposal—not a gift but "at his disposal." Ed has never been in academic difficulty, yet he knows that any professor who would fail him for a semester would find himself in trouble, not only with the alumni, but with the administration as well.

Ed asked me if I knew how much the gate receipts at Kingston were during a single season. It had never occurred to me to ask. When the team plays five games at home, apparently the take is over $700,000. This money, aside from the cut for visiting teams, is plowed back into football expenses: salaries for ten coaches; a special fund for recruiting; uniforms, expenses for trips, upkeep of stadium, etc. There have been years when, although the receipts were just as high, the college—out of a special fund—had to make up a deficit!

At this stage of its development, according to Ed, Kingston does not need a greater reputation for power football. It desperately needs a reputation for preparing men and women to make the grade in medicine, law, the ministry, music, architecture, science, government, education, social work, and so on. This, he says, is what a college education is all about; it should have nothing to do with turning out gladiators who maul each other for temporary glory.

As for myself, I am hung up on football. I see every Kingston game at home and away. On weekends, I compulsively watch two or three professional games on television. So you can understand that I share some of your disappointment in Ed's decision. However, I hope you will not let this destroy your solid relation with your son. The two of you have something far more valuable than football.

Sincerely,
W. S.

They're All Alike

DEAR MR. GRABOWSKI,

I know the struggle you have had in accepting today's youth. Ed's decision has not made it any easier for you. The generation gap is great, but it has been made so by what you call the criminal element in youth—the beards, the long hair, the sex libertines, and the pot pushers.

I want to try to explain to you how I read the young people of today. This is not to argue with you or attempt a rationalization of the behavior we encounter everywhere we turn. I do it simply to let you know my position. Perhaps then you can tell where you and I agree and disagree.

It seems to me that there are four distinct groups among us, and there is a greater gap between these young people than there is between them and their elders. There may be "cross-overs"—certain youngsters who find themselves in two or more of these groups. But in the main I believe the lines are sharply drawn. If the religious, educational, and political leaders of our day cannot distinguish between them, the future of this country is dim indeed—we've had it.

First, there is a criminal element, the "youth Mafia." These are young people from all walks of life—rich and poor, black and white—who, for a variety of sociological and psychological reasons, live by the criminal code. They steal, assault, rape, and if necessary kill to get their kicks or get ahead. Bribery and extortion among high-school and college students across the nation is as widespread as it is in the worlds of business, finance, and politics. These young people do not fight the system; they have joined it, and they are determined to make it work for them as it works for their elders.

Second, there are the outwardly clean-cut young Americans who are exploited by their elders on radio, television, and in the press. They sing patriotic songs and wave the flag, and with gusto they mouth the platitudes of the older generation. They do not think of challenging either the laws or customs that have been handed down to them. They conform in such matters as dress, language, music, and morals. Yet for many of them the ideals of democracy simply do not exist; in fact they literally do not even know what those ideals are. Democracy for them has something to do with the "American way of life," with getting ahead, with marrying well and keeping things as they are. These kids care nothing about the unjust and immoral killing in Zantusi. Our government has decided we should be there—why query such a policy? To question the decision and our subsequent intervention in a small African country is to be "unpatriotic." (Whereas, if in truth we have made a colossal blunder, then *not* to question and challenge it is in fact unpatriotic in the extreme.)

These young people care nothing about conditions that result in the exploitation of the unlettered and the unrepresented. They do not know, they do not care, they do not believe that thousands of helpless children exist in *this* country in a state of starvation. They do not care that there is blatant discrimination against many who are denied homes, jobs, and the ballot for no reason other than the color of their skin.

Yet they wave the flag and sing their patriotic songs. At an early age they were taught to conform, and this they do with comfortable ease. I have seen them not only on television and in the press but here at Kingston, but I am convinced that the wave of the future is not with them. They lack initiative, imagination, and compassion. Frustrated and often embittered, they simply go through the motions of getting ahead and making good.

Third, the hippies and the beatniks. There is supposed to be a difference between them but I fail to see it. The hippie is said to be the flower child, the beatnik the ultimate cynic, but one thing both have in common is their withdrawal from society. They reject, despise, and hate us. In my judgment, their emotional hang-up with this culture is so great that they will never in numbers return to the fold. They will never make a significant contribution to the life of *their* generation. In the midst of their filth, drugs, and disease, their disillusionment and despair, they have nothing to give but their emptiness. Hippies and beatniks are often pictured as happy and carefree, but I have found them the saddest people among us. The notion among some of our liberals that these juvenile derelicts have something to say or something to give, or that in some mysterious way they are equipped to act in judgment upon society, is nonsense. They crave nothing but irresponsibility and all the "bread"— money, that is—they can get their hands on.

Fourth, are the young people full of hope, ideals, and enthusiasm who want a piece of the action now. For the most part, they are nonconformist in dress, haircuts, music, and dance. Many of them (not all) have also rejected certain forms of religion, especially of worship. They see no sense in our solemn assemblies where God is complimented and placated but where the needs of people are ignored or forgotten. Some in this group have also, to a certain extent, quietly renounced the sex mores of the older generation. By "quietly" I mean they do not communicate this to their parents: "Look, Pop, see what

I'm doing—" However, many feel the sham and unreality in the older generation more keenly at the point of sex than at any other place in our society. These serious young people are determined to break, once and for all, from the hypocritical and unreal pronouncements of their elders and to live their lives by their own sex codes. This does not necessarily mean that they are libertines or that they are amoral; it means that the old rules of the game are no longer their rules—they are establishing their own codes.

Although we may have trouble completely accepting many of their actions, these serious and involved young people represent the wave of the future. They are solid, they are real. They are not hung up on dope, and they do not believe in violence, though they strongly believe in agitation and struggle. Many of them are willing to practice civil disobedience to change an unjust law or to right a wrong. They get their kicks not from dope but from positive, creative, justice-inspired acion. In this last group I put Ed Grabowski. College-age men and women such as Ed represent the best and perhaps the last hope of a free and responsible society in the U.S.A.

So the struggle is on. Forgive my lecture! Our religious, educational, and political leaders cannot continue to ignore this group of alert, committed young people. If they do, they will succeed only in bringing the temple down around all our heads, and will be remembered in history for their blindness and stupidity.

May God give us the sense and good judgment to encourage *these* young people and let them in.

Sincerely,
W. S.

We Have Created Madness and Call It Peace

DEAR MR. GRABOWSKI,

I am glad you had a chance to come to Kingston and talk to Ed. You can see his mind is made up.

Why did he wait until the middle of the season, just before the Dartmouth game, to announce his step? I asked him this. He wanted a way, he said, to dramatize his decision—to get as much publicity as possible, not for himself, but for the cause of humanity which he now feels he represents. If this is what he wanted, he certainly got it. As you know newspaper reporters and columnists all over the country have featured his dramatic departure, and each has published his own interpretation of the reasons he did it. One wrote that Ed was dying of leukemia, another that he was still grieving over the loss of his mother, another, that he could not stay academically eligible, another that he had had a fight with Coach Stew Baker, another that he was having a nervous breakdown and simply could not function. Ed was interviewed yesterday by a reporter for a New York paper. He said, "Intercollegiate football is a big come-on; I want no further part of it. There are more important things to do. Each of us has only one time around. I want my life to count for something."

Of all the reporters writing on Ed's defection, this was the only one who believed him. We are so saturated with the American goals of success, glory, and gain that when an unambiguous, self-sacrificing decision is made, we will not and cannot accept it.

While the Dartmouth game was being played, Ed took off

for Michigan, where he joined thousands of college students who are actively involved in national politics. He is concerneu about the crises in our cities, but the foremost problem for him is the war in Zantusi. This intervention in a civil war has sapped our national strength, created rampant inflation, divided our people, siphoned off funds that should have been used in critical domestic areas. Ed now believes that the military-industrial complex is the greatest internal threat to our existence as a democracy. The federal budget allocates 8o per cent of our country's income for military and space expenditures. The morale of the nation was never lower; the spirit and unity of our people have been in some way broken. He feels that young people must not perpetuate the errors and wrongs of their elders, nor can they continue to take handouts from their parents or from the government without giving something in return. The political power centers of this nation must be reached, redirected, and redeemed. Ed has found something to which he can give himself without reservation.

You met Mrs. Spires. Quite an attractive young lady, don't you think? As you can see, she too is militant. She feels that the hope of the nation is in its young people, the "new youth" as she calls them. Professor Spires has undoubtedly made a deep impression on Ed, but I hope you will not feel too harsh toward her. She is not only an attractive and outgoing person, but a brilliant social and political analyst.

In addition to Mrs. Spires, several other factors fostered Ed's decision. Dr. Martin Luther King, Jr. came to Kingston several months before his assassination. In a speech delivered before the student body, he said that in recent years he had carefully considered two questions: "Can this nation be saved?" and "Is it worth saving?" He finally decided in the affirmative: this nation could be saved and was worth saving. But, he said, it will not be changed for the better by those who resort to violence and bloodshed, or those who hate and have rejected it, or those who in despair throw up their hands and do nothing. It can and will be saved by those who have the dream of a strong, decent, and just society, and who are willing to struggle and pay with their lives if necessary for the fulfillment of that dream.

This address had a profound effect on Ed. The assassination further ignited his spirit.

In addition to such experiences, under the direction of Mrs. Spires he has been doing quite a bit of reading. He brought a book to my office the other day. In it was a selection written by the famous runaway slave, Frederick Douglass. Douglass was born in 1817 and escaped to freedom in 1838. Since I had never read anything that Douglass wrote, Ed wanted me not only to read it but to copy and file it for personal use. So here is what the former slave said:

> If there is no struggle, there is no progress. Those who pro-fess to favor freedom, and yet deprecate agitation, are men who want crops without plowing up the ground. They want rain without thunder and lightning. They want the ocean without the awful roar of its many waters. This struggle may be a moral one, or it may be a physical one; or it may be both moral and physical; but it must be a struggle. Power concedes nothing without demand. It never did and it never will. Men may not get all they pay for in this world; but they certainly pay for all they get.

Ed will not wait for graduation. He is ready now to enter the struggle and to become more deeply involved in the press-ing problems of his day. He has exchanged the motto, "Go Get'em Wildcats!" for that of an ancient Greek: "I live to help tame the savagery of man and make gentle the life of the world."

You could not quite hide your horror when you saw your son in his Nehru jacket and the peace medallion around his neck!

I can't interpret precisely what this attire signifies, except to say that I believe it is more than a fad—it is symbolic of a desire to change the old ways. Though I would feel uncomfortable in such garb, my assistant Chaplain Croy wears nothing but "peace" and "mod" clothes. By the way, he and Ed hit it off real well. But I must say again that it is neither I nor Chaplain Croy who has most impressed your son. That person is Hazel Spires. Incidentally, I would be interested in knowing how you feel about her. It seemed to me that during the dinner at the hotel you found her charming.

If there are further developments at this end of the line, I will let you know.

Sincerely,
W. S.

Those Who Hunger and Thirst After Freedom

DEAR MR. GRABOWSKI,

I am sorry I did not get to see you when you were on campus last week. Ed says that even though you were here for two days he saw very little of you. Your time seemed to be reserved for the attractive Mrs. Spires! Joking aside—that pleases me. There is nothing like springtime to bring out the sentimental in us.

Another school year is coming to an end. Since this year has been unusually hectic, I am looking forward to the summer. My wife and I are at last getting a long-delayed trip to England. The British, for the most part, appear to be tolerant of our blundering in world affairs. Afer all, they were the kingpins of the world for a long time and probably made bloopers as big as our own. My British friends, though never publicly saying so, appear to be trying to convey something like "Cheer up, old friends! We know the embarrassment and humiliation you feel because of your government's excesses in world affairs. We, too, have been there."

Ed has become good friends with a student in his class by the name of Larry Erickson. You may have heard of him. He is editor of the *Kingstonian* and has led most of the student demonstrations on campus this year. Ed admires Larry quite a bit, and the two of them will be working for a "peace" senator in Washington this summer.

I can answer your urgent question without reservations. Ed has not become a Communist, a Communist dupe, or a pinko. In fact, he holds certain views that might put him in the conservative camp. For instance, he is opposed to this nation's bureaucratic welfare programs. He is eloquent about how city, state, and federal programs overlap, and welfare workers get in each other's way as they direct, control, and manipulate their subjects. For he has seen this comedy of errors as he tried to work with some of the poverty programs in Kingston county. Ed feels that a guaranteed annual income to all families who could qualify would be much more sensible than the dole or welfare assistance. He insists that this could be handled on a reverse income tax plan. (I am giving you just a sketch of his present ideas.) Everyone would file a tax form. Those whose annual income falls within a certain amount—tied to the cost of living—would receive money rather than paying money to the government. There would be no checking and no policing of citizens on how their money is spent. Well—who can say? A few years ago this would have seemed a very drastic idea.

Ed also feels that the test of a free economy is in its ability to provide jobs for all those who can and should work. If the economy cannot do this it soon will destroy itself; therefore the federal government should be prepared to offer jobs to all who want to work. And the work should not be menial, but should be meaningful, necessary, and remunerative. There is nothing more degrading than working day after day at an empty, artificial job.

Ed is quite excited about a lecture given by Mrs. Spires yesterday morning about government farm restrictions in a world of famine. Even in our country people starve for want of food, but millions upon millions perish—actually die of starvation—in countries abroad. Yet our subsidized and often wealthy farmers must allow machinery and land to remain idle. The amount of food this country could produce, if incentives were present and restrictions lifted, is not known, but it would certainly be astronomical! This nation has within its power to provide basic food to all our people and at the same time feed the entire world, if necessary. It cannot do so because the subsidized and controlled farmer must remain idle rather than plant.

Is Ed a Communist, you ask. He is everything else but a Communist! Communism in the world today is in many ways a dead issue, I think. It is dead, broken, fragmented, and stalemated. Communist leaders have turned their energies to maintaining their own airtight, oppressive totalitarian regimes, their Communist parties in all countries are ruled by stiff, conservative older men who frantically try to "keep things as they are." Afraid of youth, afraid of change, afraid of the future, they struggle to hold the people in check. An excellent illustration of this is the intervention of Soviet troops in Czechoslovakia. The people of Czechoslovakia were not at odds with Russia over how to earn money or the ownership of property. No, the people craved their civil liberties. They want the privilege of free expression, to speak, to write, to assemble, to discuss, to worship, to sing and to make love. The old men of the Kremlin, steeped in their orthodoxy and supported by military power, would not tolerate this. It appears that the "military mentality" is the same the world over. If there are serious problems between nations, there is only one way to solve them and that is by tanks, guns, and jets. Will orthodox, conservative military men never learn that some problems between nations are exacerbated rather than healed by military means?

Mr. Grabowski, I call your attention to one thing in connection with the Soviet intervention in Czechoslovakia. Remember the pictures of people in Prague sitting or lying down in the streets before the mighty Russian tanks? Who were these people? Not old men and old women, not men and women your age and mine. They were long-haired high-school and college-age young people! A number of them were killed or maimed by those tanks. They are the same young people who, in this land of ours, cry out for freedom and justice for all. These are the young people who are saying loud and clear that grinding poverty cannot exist side by side in the same country and in the same neighborhood with extravagance and affluence; they are saying that they will no longer tolerate a government that pays people not to produce food while millions starve. These are the young people most feared by some of our political leaders. And they are mistakenly labeled "hippies" and "beatniks."

At first I was as shocked as you when Ed made the great leap and gave up a football career. I guess I'm still square enough to let the "Rah-rah!" spirit of college athletics get to me. But now I'm really pretty excited about Ed and what his life can accomplish in the great cause of humanity. He'll pay a big price for the decision he made, but the rewards, in terms of internal satisfaction, will be much greater.

The next time you are on campus, see the Professor but save a little time for me.

Sincerely,

W. S.

When the Pressure Is Applied

DEAR MR. GRABOWSKI,

This note is to say that I appreciate your efforts on behalf of Dean Tom Blower. In spite of several restrictive ideas, he is a good man. The position of the deanship is impossible. Various power groups, including the Board of Trustees, faculty, alumni, student body, and the administration must be dealt with and often pacified. You did an excellent job with the New York Alumni Club. They applied the pressure where it counted the most. As a result the Dean has been saved, not only from embarrassment but from academic extinction.

When I return from Northwestern next week, I will fill you in on the details. Until then, I am

Sincerely yours,
W. S.

Damned If You Do and Damned If You Don't

DEAR MR. GRABOWSKI,

The situation about Dean Blower is a little complicated, but I will try to explain it. In recent months he has shown some signs of a liberal spirit, especially in dealing with students. Though at the time he said little, he was in favor of liberalizing the rules in connection with the use of rooms in the girls' dorms. He is also in favor of greater student involvement in such things as formulation of the curriculum. It is now generally known that he is opposed to fraternities and sororities. For these and other reasons, the Dean has become a target for various groups on and off campus. The time appeared right for them to move in and demand his resignation.

The situation was complicated by the activities of certain students who are members of Kingston's strongest fraternities. As you know, the SL house at Kingston is one of the largest and most beautiful on campus. Beginning early in the first semester, the men did a foolish and unnecessary thing, and they did it for kicks—just to be different. Each weekend they brought six call girls up from New York to entertain forty-eight men. The girls stayed in the house Friday and Saturday nights and returned to New York on Sunday. One of the assistant deans got wind of it, notified the President, and SL was permanently suspended and the house closed. It would never again operate on the Kingston campus.

The men were forced to find lodging elsewhere. As you know, living quarters at Kingston and in the city are at a premium. In the light of the hardship on the men, the house was reopened, but it remained under suspension. At this point, three millionaire Kingston alumni, each a devoted SL and each a generous contributor to the college, spoke a gentle word to the President. "Boys will be boys," they said. Closing the house and *permanent* suspension was too harsh. The house was already reopened; why not make the suspension for sixty days? This was done. SL is back in business and they have promised "No more call girls." The Dean opposed the reinstatement and hence incurred the anger of the fraternity students as well as several important SL alumni.

The situation concerning Dean Blower was further complicated by the "radical liberal" element on the faculty. They, too, wanted the Dean eliminated and demanded his resignation.

He favored retaining compulsory chapel, and he has taken a fairly hard line on the war. I discovered, to my own chagrin, that liberals (especially "pacifist liberals") can be as violent and irrational as reactionaries. If you disagree with them on one point, they dismiss or banish you. According to their tally, you must be "liberal" on all points or you are a dead duck. There is no intolerance so rank as liberal intolerance. These radical liberals threatened a faculty strike if Dean Blower were not immediately ousted.

Several of us, not enthusiastic supporters of Blower but nevertheless sympathetic to him, sensed the situation and were determined to do something about it. Unknown to the Dean, I went to several young "liberal" professors and told them that they were playing directly into the hands of the ultraconservative, reactionary elements on the Board of Trustees and among the alumni, faculty, and student body. For a number of years Dr. Angus Lowdin, chairman of the Department of Business Administration, has been anxious to become the Dean of Liberal Arts. What a travesty! He has played his cards well and it seemed as if he might pull it off. Lowdin was an old man at twenty-one; he has no contact with students of this generation or with younger faculty members. He would have tried to set in motion prehistoric disciplinary actions and programs. In my judgment, if Blower had been ousted and Lowdin appointed, Kingston would have been torn by violent demonstrations, protests, and even riots. Lowdin simply does not know or care about the feelings of students. He is not interested in discovering who they are, what they want, or the level of their intelligence. On the other hand, Dean Tom Blower is an excellent academician; he knows students and is sympathetic to them and also sensitive to the problems of younger faculty members. He has one or two blind spots—but who hasn't?

The tragedy was averted, thanks to you, the New York

Alumni Club, and several other alumni clubs over the country. You did your part in the field. Some of us were forced to resort to power politics on campus. I called Ed to my office and explained to him exactly what was in the works. I asked him if he could get a number of key students to help stop the "dump Blower" drive. He mentioned Larry Erickson, editor of the *Kingstonian* and several other influential students. Ed felt that once the students knew that a Blower resignation meant a Lowdin take-over, they would act. Ed, Larry, and a girl by the name of Sue Blanton went directly to the President and laid it on the line—Dean Blower must stay. With several teams working, hundreds of names were secured on a petition. These were sent to the trustees, who were markedly impressed. In this day, when college students are demanding the ouster of presidents, vice presidents, and deans, they thought it was a healthy sign that Kingston students were lending such enthusiastic support to their dean!

A personal word. I take my hat off to you for the marvelous way you have stuck by Ed. I admire you more than any parent I know, for being so determined not to allow a difference of opinion to drive a wedge between you and your son. He is no longer a great football hero, but a man in his own right.

Thanks again for what you did for Dean Blower.

Sincerely,

W. S.

White Racism Will Not Listen

Dear Mr. Grabowski,

Your call this morning at 2:30 caught me in a stupor, and I am not sure I made sense on the phone.

I have just come from the hospital. Ed is being detained another day for observation. He has bruises on his body, a split lip and a gash above the left eye. The doctors assure me that there are no internal injuries. He will be released tomorrow.

It is rather ironical that you had just about reached the place where you could accept Negroes as human beings when this incident occurred. I hope you will not let it destroy your faith in your black brothers. During the past year Ed has learned one of the most important lessons of life: i.e., if you love, you do not always get love in return. As you know, he has been working with young Negro boys in the afternoons and on Sunday. His work has taken him into the worst ghetto in Kingston, not far from the college. In recent weeks his presence there has infuriated a number of extremists in the black power movement. These people hate "whitey"—they want racial separation, and many of them believe in violence. The white man, they feel, got all he possesses through violence, and it is by violence that he retains it. This particular black man feels that only through violence can he ever hope to achieve a favored place in the sun. Ed's presence in the ghetto was not only an act of condescension but a real threat to their leadership of their own boys.

They warned him to stay out of the neighborhood, but he refused. Yesterday afternoon three young Negro men jumped him and beat him to the ground with clubs. Some of the boys with whom he has been working ran for the police, and Ed was saved from permanent injury or death. I checked with several bystanders and they say it was an amazing sight to see this huge, muscular young giant being beaten and offering no resistance. If he had been so minded, he probably could have throttled all three of his assailants.

Ed's version, as he explained it in the hospital this morning, made me ashamed not so much of the blacks as of the stupid whites who have driven these extremists to savagery. Through a torn lip he said, "White racism did this."

He kept going over the reasons, as if he couldn't stop. For more than two hundred years the white man held the black man a slave in this country. He was bought, sold, and bred like cattle. Then for more than a century he has been oppressed through open and hidden forms of segregation and discrimination. America with its rich and wonderful life was denied to him, even after Lincoln's proclamation "freed" him. During all these ugly years the white man raped his women, denied education to his children, allowed him only substandard medical services—or no medical services at all, refused him the ballot, prevented him from acquiring a job or buying a pleasant home. The power structure of the white man—the police, the courts, the armed forces—kept him out of schools, hotels, motels, restaurants, and theaters. To this day he is denied the privilege of worshiping God in most churches.

The more anybody sympathized with Ed or denounced his attackers, the more he said, painfully, "No—no! you don't understand—" and tried to explain. Until recently the Negro gave some evidence that he believed, not in the dignity and beauty of his blackness, but in his inferiority. Then, not more than a dozen or so years ago, he came out fighting. He is now determined that if he and his people cannot have the good things provided by this country, nobody is going to have them. He will disrupt transportation, burn the cities, and make living intolerable for us all. He no longer cringes in fear; his motto has become, "Burn, baby, burn!" and "Kill, baby, kill!"

This, according to Ed, is what blind, stupid white racism has brought about in our midst. He said slowly and sadly, "It took us three hundred years to create it, but at last we have brought it into full bloom." He is right, I'm afraid, and what is worse, we must live with it for a long time to come.

What I would like you, my friend, to understand is that there are a great number of blacks in our midst who are *not* extremists—they do *not yet* believe that violence is the only way. Like our responsible young people, they want to participate in the social and political life of the nation. If we ever let them "in," it will be a new day for our country.

I asked Ed if he intended to return to the ghetto. He smiled crookedly and said, "I'll be there Monday afternoon. The children need me and they want me."

What a guy!

Sincerely,
W. S.

Lead, Kindly Light

DEAR MR. GRABOWSKI,

These are happy days for you!

Ed deserved his graduation honors. It was a joy to hear the standing ovation he got during the commencement exercises. Such outbursts have become more or less a thing of the past, but the custom was revived, irresistibly, for a worthy person. To think that he's headed for the Divinity School to study for the ministry—not politics, as many of his friends expected, but the parish ministry! For he tells me he doesn't want to prepare for one of the exciting "specialized ministries" outside the church, but for the *parish ministry*. He knows I have mixed feelings about the parish, but this in no way dims our relationship.

The organized church in our time, I feel, has almost lost its soul. It has so often become an instrument of man's greed and selfishness, a way to satisfy his insatiable lust for power in both high places and low. And it has become in many ways irrelevant and irresponsible to the age in which it lives. I'd say that two points, among others, illustrate this: first, the church in this country, after long turmoil, is still the most segregated institution in American life. Of course there are "integrated" churches, but the fact remains that the black man is denied membership in most churches, not simply in the South but in various parts of the country. Maybe American history will one day deny this, and no one living two or three hundred years from now will believe it! But, for the record, we must confess in shame and horror that this is today's church.

My second point in the irrelevance and irresponsibility of the church is the Pope's encyclical on birth control. This glaringly reveals how far the church and some of its clergy are removed from the needs and desires of people. The Pope could just as well have been speaking from another planet, so far removed is he from his own people. But let not Protestants take comfort in this tragi-comic stroke of irrelevance—Protestants, especially in the United States, with their loud, vociferous pronouncements on drink, divorce, dancing, lewdness, hemlines, etc., have been and still are issuing Vatican ultimatums of their own. Of course, I suppose most Roman Catholics will pay no more attention to the Pope's edict than Protestants have to their clergy's pietistic pronouncements.

But the contemporary parish still offers a man of strength, intelligence, and commitment, a chance to invest his life in both people and issues. No man in society is closer to people in the crises of living and dying than the parish minister; and, believe it or not, no man can really exercise more influence on the issues of the day. He does this both directly and indirectly. The minister does not have to be irrelevant and "other-worldly"; he can be a strength to his people and the voice of conscience in the community.

Ed will be a good minister, I am sure. He will live with the deadly preacher image and won't bow to the "religious establishment"; I doubt very much if he will yield to the demands of social and ecclesiastical conformity. He will be a good minister because he cares about people and the tangible problems of the day. As an undergraduate he has demonstrated his willingness to pay the price, not simply for talking—that is, preaching—but for acting. In fact, your son possesses a priceless quality, very rare today, and that is *moral courage*.

As you know, Ed has come a long way in these four years. He came to Kingston a boy with little faith in God and no church affiliation. He is leaving determined to be a minister of God. He told me the other day that his favorite Scripture was the announcement of Jesus when he identified himself, not with the establishment, but with the needs of people: "The Spirit of the Lord is upon me, because He anointed me to preach good tidings to the poor; He hath sent me to proclaim release to the captives, and recovering of sight to the blind, to set at liberty them that are bruised, to proclaim the acceptable year of the Lord."

Ed is becoming a parish minister when most young men, including students in our seminaries and divinity schools, consider the parish a meaningless vocation. He is aiming at the local parish when hundreds of older men my age, both Protestant and Catholic, are severing all ties with the church. Some of them do enter related fields of endeavor, such as teaching or the poverty program, but many renounce their vocation to seek secular positions. I know you had hoped and planned that one day Ed would take over your business. But in a very fine way you have accepted his turning his back on football and the world of business. I know you will accept his studying for the ministry also.

You ask me to comment on your attire at commencement. I

can only say that on you the Nehru jacket looks great! The peace medallion is certainly not out of place; it gives your outfit a ring of authenticity. You have joined the masses of our non-conforming but responsible young people. Why not go all the way?

Of course I'll plan to be present at the wedding. You know by now that by winning the lovely Mrs. Spires you have captured the prize of the year. Count me in—I'll be there for both the wedding and the reception.

Sincerely,
W. S.

II
To Major and Mrs. Rivers,
concerning their daughter Hope

College Ruined Our Daughter

Dear Major and Mrs. Rivers,

You ask in your letter, "What kind of a school are you trying to be at Kingston?"

I have asked myself that question more than once. At times I feel we are a liberal arts college striving to acquaint young men and women with their world, past and present, and to help them not only to survive but to live in freedom. We are helping them move from the world of adolescence to the world of maturity.

At other times I feel we are running a top-grade junior high school. Faculty members, even in the same departments, split, divide, squabble, and fight over minute details such as promotions, department chairmen, and so on. The question of whether the college would begin this fall's schedule the first or second week in September precipitated a hassle last year that lasted for months. And of course there is the constant five-cornered power struggle between administration, faculty, student body, alumni, and trustees.

The junior-high-school aspect is most evident in our dealing with students. I ask you, to what extent can the college be "parents" to a student? Many students come here from high schools where, since the age of sixteen, they have driven their own cars (cars at Kingston are barred for freshmen and sophomores). Most of them have had a certain amount of freedom in connection with hours, dress, dating, and so on, but here, until recently, restrictions have been severe. The college has tried to act as "parents in absentia," and in doing so has often succeeded only in making itself look foolish.

We have several students like Hope who have come from a strict family and church background. The few liberties available

45

at Kingston are like strong wine to the inexperienced. They cannot handle even a minimum of freedom; they are at a loss to make decisions without the multiple rules and regulations set as guide lines for them by Mom and Dad and the church. Thus to some students and parents we are too old-fashioned; to others we are "loose and decadent."

I have taken the occasion to explain some of the internal problems at Kingston because of your letter to the chairman of the Board of Trustees, a copy of which was enclosed in your letter to me. In that letter you state:

When our daugher, Hope, left Memphis and entered Kingston College more than three years ago, she was a fine Christian girl. She went to church and Sunday School every Sunday, she read her Bible every day, she did not drink or smoke, and she scarcely dated at all. Now her life has been ruined by her associations at Kingston. She never goes to church or Sunday School, she never reads her Bible, she drinks and smokes, and we have reason to believe she goes out with boys beneath her social standing.

We thought Kingston was a fine school, but it has ruined our daughter. She took a course in religion which destroyed her faith in the Bible, a course in philosophy which destroyed her faith in God, a course in psychology which destroyed her faith in her parents, a course in biology which destroyed her faith in divine creation, and a course in political science which destroyed her faith in the American way of life.

You describe how she was converted at the age of twelve in a revival meeting conducted by the famous evangelist Johnny Lester, and how she did the things necessary to deepening the spiritual life. I have nothing against Dr. Lester except to say that it has been my observation that in many instances his formula for strengthening the "spiritual life" does not work. I wonder if he is altogether clear as to what spiritual life is. Sometimes I get the impression that Dr. Lester thinks spiritual life is strengthened and improved by observing certain rituals which he feels are in some way related to God. It apparently never occurs to him that spiritual life is the life of love as it relates to the human family, a denial of self in the interest of simple justice. The parable of the sheep and goats should settle this matter once and for all.

In closing your letter, you ask me the question, "As the chaplain, what can you do for our daughter?"

I must state frankly that at the moment I feel that I can render little assistance to Hope. Perhaps someone else can get to her, but not I. She comes by my office quite frequently, but never for a friendly chat or to have a question answered or to seek help. She comes by to get me "told." She is always argumentative and combative. I, the chaplain, am part of the "establishment." I am the symbol of a rotten society. Past thirty, I am over the hill. I have not had a new idea in years. I do not understand young people, especially college students. According to Hope, we adults have created a world that stinks—reeks with middle-class corruption—and the perfume of plausibility with which we spray society only makes the smell worse. The only thing for young people to do is to reject society, separate themselves from it, and wish it immediate damnation.

She will sometimes breeze into my office, put bare feet on my desk, blow cigarette smoke in my face, laugh, and say, "Chaplain, you've had it. You're just like my mother and father. They don't know what it's all about, and I know damn well you don't know what it's all about."

I will continue to be as patient as possible. If the opening comes, if Hope ever needs and wants assistance, you can count on me to do my best.

You asked about Sue Blanton and Hope's association with her. The newspaper account of Sue's demonstrations and arrest were somewhat exaggerated. I am positive that Hope and Sue are not friends. They have nothing in common and they live in two different worlds. I doubt that, except for an occasional class together, the girls ever see each other.

With kindest regards and wishing that I could be of more help, I am

Sincerely,
W. S.

Totalitarian

Dear Major Rivers,

Dean Blower has forwarded to me your letter demanding that I be fired. He has asked me to answer it.

During my tenure at Kingston I have had a variety of relationships with parents, some pleasant and some less so. It has been a long time since I have taken as much abuse from anyone as I have from you.

In your letter to the Dean you refer to me as a "phony intellectual," a "stupid left-winger," a "dirty bastard," and a "goddam pacifist." I may be all of these things except the bastard; I am pretty sure this is not the case.

Your resentment seems to have two points of focus: you charge that I have led demonstrations against the war and that I directed the fight to remove ROTC from the campus. I can set the record straight on both counts. I am opposed to the present war in Africa; I feel it is the most colossal blunder in foreign affairs that our government ever made, greater than Vietnam. But thus far, due to a lack of courage or perhaps lack of faith in the technique, I have led no demonstrations or protests of any kind. Regrettably, to this date I have done nothing but write and talk.

In this connection I must say that I am no pacifist. As long as evil, selfish, and violent men are in the world, a nation, I feel, needs its armed forces for much the same reasons as it needs its police force. I wish this were a planet where police power was never necessary, where we could live without locking doors, and all men could trust each other. But this is not the case, and to imagine that it is or soon could be demands an interpretation of the nature of man which is to say the least naïve.

Therefore, the use of power by a city or a nation must be responsible. The question is not whether force under certain circumstances will be used, but whether it will be used responsibly. It is not a responsible use of force when Soviet troops intervene in Czechoslovakia to put down the surge of the people for the right to enjoy and express civil liberties. It is not a responsible use of power when our government sends 40,-000 troops into the little country of the Dominican Republic, there to support with jets and tanks an uprising against a constitutionally elected government—the only constitutionally elected government that republic had seen for many years. In that instance, our government would have been justified in going to the assistance of the existing, democratically elected government rather than the insurgent rebellion of the military junta. (Nevertheless, we managed to stumble and fumble our way out of that blunder with a minimum amount of embarrassment and world censure.) So I am no pacifist. I really do believe that an imperfect world demands the use of force; but it must be *responsible* force. Responsible use of military power will be more likely when the elected civilian authorities, including the President, are not unduly influenced by the high command. I do not feel that the present war represents a responsible use of force.

Now concerning the ROTC on campus. As I said, I have led no demonstration to remove this military installation from our campus, though I am opposed to its being here. The reason for my opposition is simple: any phase of military life, by its very nature, is contradictory to virtually everything a liberal arts college attempts to do. *It is perfected totalitarianism.* Power in the chain of command and secrecy in its operations must exist in any effective military system. After the Russian Revolution, when the Communists took over, there was a brief period when the military was "democratized." Officers were no different from privates, everyone was buddy-buddy, with the results that the army soon became chaotic. Needless to say, that experiment in a democratic army was short-lived. The military, in order to do its job, must be a fascist type of totalitarianism, and that is precisely what it is in every major country in the world.

In contrast, by its own nature, the liberal arts college attempts to create a world marked by free inquiry, free and open dissent, free and responsible decisions, and internal (autonomous) discipline. It often does not succeed in living by these principles, but they are both the air the college breathes and the goals it is striving to reach. The military must be opposed per se to all four of these concepts. For instance, it cannot tolerate free inquiry into the "rightness" or "wrongness" of an ideological position other than that held by the nation it seeks to defend. In other words, an examination of first principles cannot be permitted. The military must dogmatically assume that "our" position is "right."

The military cannot encourage free and open dissent. Free debate and nonviolent dissent are necessary to the functioning of democracy. The right of any group, large or small, to assemble peacefully to redress grievances is an American constitutional right. The responsible and constitutional use of power involves the protection of those who are dissenting, *not of those who are attempting to prevent dissent*.

In the military, however, an officer or enlisted man who disagrees with a policy established by those higher up must keep his mouth shut and obey or be held for a serious violation of discipline.

It is also obvious that the military cannot permit free decisions on the part of its personnel. This would result in immediate chaos. Servicemen are not free to decide how long they will serve, where they will serve, the kind of work they will do, or under whom they will work. They must live under the absolute control of the chain of command. Discipline must likewise be imposed from above. In fact, all major activity is dictated from "above." A serviceman who ignored these regulations and sought to follow a self-discipline dictated by his own reason and conscience would be a menace to his fellow soldiers. The best soldier is one who does what he is told and does not ask questions. The more totalitarian the system, the more efficiently it operates.

The ROTC is an important arm of the military. As such it stands in direct opposition to what a liberal arts college is attempting to do. It must oppose free inquiry, free and open dissent, free and responsible decisions, and autonomous discipline. It must live in an atmosphere of secrecy and censorship. This mentality destroys man's creativity and stifles the expression of both conscience and reason. In general, the American way of life has envisaged for its citizens a state of freedom from such coercions as normally prevail in an army, and has understood them as dangerous to the principles of democracy if made to apply to the normal life of citizens. Therefore I am opposed not only to compulsory military training for students on our campus—which existed until a few years ago—but even to the ROTC being on campus on either a conscripted or a voluntary basis.

I feel pretty sure that some day, in the future, the clumsy and unfair draft system will be discarded. In its place, a well-paid professional army will emerge. When this day arrives, officers for such an army will be properly trained in military tactics at such academies across the country as are deemed necessary by the high command. Candidates for these schools will be men who thrive better in a totalitarian system than in a free and open society. I hope, however, that in our democratic society the military will not grow any bigger in numbers and financial power than it now is. There is a point of no return when what we meant as a defense becomes the tyrant in our midst.

You indicate in your letter to the Dean that you are leaving immediately for Zantusi, and that there you will fight Communism and thus make it possible for "crackpots such as your chaplain" to live in freedom. To date a civil war is going on in that country. Our high command now says it is unlikely that we can gain a military victory over the guerillas. In the light of this, it appears to me that the best way to fight communism is to make the American dream a reality alike in goods, services, and civil liberties. This must be done for all people on our own shores, and I believe it must not stop there. Foreign aid, in terms of greater technical and economic assistance, must be given to those peoples who give some indication that they want our help and who prefer an open society to a closed one.

You should know by now, Major Rivers, that we do not fight totalitarian communism with tanks and jets; we fight it with the overproduction of the abundant life. We can keep a Communist nation at bay with the threat of the atomic bomb, but we cannot fight communism with bombs. When goods and services exist, not for the privileged but for all—when civil liberties are in a healthy state, including free speech, free worship, and free assembly—we are successfully fighting communism. When there is no discrimination in housing, jobs, or the ballot, then totalitarianism, called by any name or "ism," becomes impotent. Many of the students I work with, those you appear to despise, are attempting to fight the totalitarian life with these weapons. I suppose we must leave the guns, tanks, and jets with men who share your point of view.

Before closing this letter, I have one suggestion of a personal nature. It concerns your daughter Hope. I know you want to see her before leaving for Africa, but I appeal to you not to come to the campus at this particular time. For the past several days she has seemed a little desperate. She keeps saying you get her "up-tight." It distresses me to say this, but she does not want to see you or talk to you. If you show up on campus, she vows she will break away from Kingston and head for San Francisco. With some students this would be an idle threat, but Hope, I feel, is telling the truth. This is her last year. In a few months she will graduate. After that no one, including Hope herself, knows what the future will be. But from my own point of view, the tragedy would be worse compounded if she left here now, without her degree, in youthful bitterness and at loose ends.

No one at the moment can reach her, not even my young and able assistant. But all of us will keep trying.

Best of wishes for a safe journey.

W. S.

The Spiritual Life

DEAR MRS. RIVERS,

Since Major Rivers left for Africa, you have communicated with President Haworth on several occasions. Your last letter to him was forwarded to me, and he has asked me to answer it. In it you say that "Chaplain Croy has had a bad influence on my daughter, Hope, and should be discharged without delay."

Your information is incorrect. Yesterday I saw Hope in front of the gym and we walked to the bookstore together. The subject of Chaplain Croy came up. Here in substance is what she said: "I can take you easier than I can Chaplain Croy. You're an honest square and he's a phony hippie." She then went into a sarcastic criticism of my assistant. "Chaplain Croy is a phony. He tries to get next to the students and win their approval. He dresses in fake clothes, with beads around his neck, and he wears a beard with long hair." His attempt to use hippie language she criticized as ludicrous: "dig," "grass," "man," etc. "If I hear him say 'man' one more time I'll scream." Then she mimicked his way of saying it.

Hope says that my assistant is first of all a preacher in hippie clothes and is trying in an underhanded way to suck some of the students into the stupid mess called Christianity. "He's the campus joke to all my friends," she says.

Chaplain Croy "in a perverted way" reminds her of Johnny Lester. Both are tall, slim, handsome, and articulate, and both are trying to win converts. Chaplain Croy does it in a sneaky way, Dr. Lester in an open and direct way. She then described for me her conversion at the revival conducted by Johnny

Lester. She said the evangelist talked about sin. She was twelve years old and Hope knew she was a sinner, she was under conviction. She had been smoking cigarettes behind the garage and she and one of the boys in the neighborhood "played around." The weight of guilt was upon her. If she publicly accepted Jesus Christ as her Savior, her sins would be forgiven and washed away—she would never have to fear death or hell again and she would go to heaven. With determination and faith she made her public profession of faith while the choir softly sang, "Where He Leads Me I Will Follow." She was later baptized and became a member of the church. For a period of a year she walked on air; she was saved and would never go to hell.

The evangelist talked a great deal about the spiritual life as opposed to the physical life. She would grow in grace by not smoking, not drinking, not dancing; by attending church and Sunday School and prayer meeting; by reading the Bible, praying every day, and "telling someone else about Jesus." She did all this, and her "spiritual life" was strengthened.

Now she says bitterly that faith was interpreted to her in terms of meaningless exercises, where you received points for legalistic behavior. The Christian life had little to do with loving people, especially those different from oneself like the Negro, the Puerto Rican, and the Mexican. It had nothing to do with a denial of self for the sake of justice.

At fourteen it happened. The "spiritual formula gave way before her perceptive mind. Hope says angrily, "It was cheap religion." Christianity asked little of her except to tell somebody else about Jesus—so she ditched it. Mrs. Rivers, I can assure you that though Hope continued to attend church, sing the songs, and listen to the sermons as long as she was in Memphis, by her present account she hated and despised every minute of it. She insists that she couldn't wait to get away from home and was determined that, once out of the influence of parents and church, she would raise hell. And this she has done. It was not Kingston College or Chaplain Croy who robbed her of faith; it was a limited, legalistic, miniature form of Christianity that did it.

You state that Hope lost her virginity at Kingston. This is apparently not the case. In her present frame of mind she would welcome the opportunity to impart to you how and under what circumstances this was accomplished at the age of fifteen. You charge that at Kingston she smoked her first marijuana cigarette. This, too, appears to be untrue, and if you catch her in one of her outbursts she will describe to you only too vividly the marijuana parties that marked her senior year in high school.

I regret that you have such a low opinion of Kingston and what we are attempting here. Believe me when I say that we are doing the best we can with what we have.

Sincerely,
W. S.

The Necessity of Discipline

DEAR MRS. RIVERS,

It is a source of disappointment to me that I have been unable to be of more help to your family. This week I received another critical and rather abusive letter from your husband in Africa.

I cannot divulge the names of Hope's close friends other than that of Fuzzy Morkowitz, whom you met briefly last year. To give you their names would simply alienate me further from

Hope and put an end to any possibility of my ever being able to help her.

The Morkowitz boy, a senior, hangs by his academic teeth, and it is possible that he will never graduate. Fuzzy has never been caught with LSD, but that he takes the trips is common knowledge around campus. As you have correctly heard, he is a regular user of marijuana and also a pusher. He was caught with the weed his freshman year and suspended for a semester. Back on campus the next year, he was wiser and more careful. Like Hope, he goes barefoot even in cold weather, and I regret to say that both of them could do with a bath. They are identified with that small irresponsible group of young people in our society who have given up on what we adults have created. They reject us and want no part of us. They laugh and sneer, but do nothing themselves to correct the abuses and injustices of society. Indeed, I think they feel that nothing can be done. So the tragedy is they live in filth and in the twilight of their drugged world.

I know it is difficult for you to understand how a child from such a home as yours could behave as Hope does. You say, "Major Rivers and I always made our children toe the mark. When they needed discipline, they got it." I would be the last to argue with you about the importance of discipline. Growing children need it as urgently as they need affection. One of the weaknesses of many modern parents, however, is the inability to be firm, consistent, and loving in applying it. Too often discipline is not only inconsistent but takes the form of self-gratification, sometimes imposed for breaking regulations that are trivial and have no meaning. Sometimes, moreover, parents discipline—that is to say, punish—their children when in reality they would like to slug each other.

I went to see the Director of Admissions about your younger

daughter Faith, and I am sorry that I have bad news for her. She cannot be accepted at Kingston, and this is not because she was expelled from Jim Jackson College. The Admissions Office investigated the expulsion and found that it was precisely as she had indicated: for a violation of the length-of-dress rule and for wearing make-up. She had completed a year and a half and had made excellent grades. But, Mrs. Rivers, Jim Jackson is not an accredited college, and the academic work Faith completed is hardly more advanced than that of a high school. I know your reservations about state junior colleges. However, if you really want her to have some sort of higher education, I advise you to begin now to get Faith enrolled in a state school for next fall. She wanted to come to Kingston but will apparently settle for a junior college even if she must begin as a freshman. If she has this much motivation, I suggest that you capitalize on it.

Hope dropped by the office today and asked if I would give her double green stamps if she attends chapel Sunday.

Sincerely,

W. S.

Everybody Needs a Lift

Dear Mrs. Rivers,

It is good to know that Faith was accepted at Lone Hill Junior College in Memphis and that you feel reconciled to her entering there next September.

Fuzzy Morkowitz has been expelled from Kingston and has returned to California. There was no chance of his graduating. I am amazed that he was able to keep his grades in passing condition for so long. As you know, Kingston admits only students who have done superior work in high school. I suppose he was a bright boy. Hope was crushed when he left and appeared to sink into deeper despair and cynicism. However, last week she attended a meeting that featured Maharishi Mahesh Yogi, and this week she gives the impression of having discovered ultimate serenity. She practices transcendental meditation twice a day and says she is being regenerated. She has accumulated piles of books and leaflets and has become quite an evangelist for the cause. She now talks to me by the hour hoping that I will see the light and come to have a true "spiritual regeneration." Indeed, she argues and debates with anyone who will listen—and some who won't.

She said to me, "After Johnny Lester, I thought I would never have faith in any preacher. But the Maharishi is something else! He's groovy, he knows the score, and he knows what spiritual life is all about."

Frankly, I am pleased that Hope has become interested in something other than the hazy world she has known for the past several years. Her health was being damaged and my worst fears for her were being confirmed. Since conversion to the faith of the Maharishi, she has touched nothing resembling a drug. She is floating on clouds of meditation—though she still needs a bath, and (since it is mid-March) ought to be wearing shoes.

As you requested, I quietly checked on her grades and credits. Her grades are better than passing. When she prepares her classwork no one knows. Her credits thus far meet all the requirements for graduation.

I asked her the other day what she wanted to do after graduation, and she replied, "Nothing—I just want to meditate and sleep."

I will answer your question in the same way that I answered Major Rivers. Your visit to Kingston at this particular time would do more harm than good. You and your daughter have had little contact with each other during these four years. For the time being Hope wishes to keep it that way. However, I suggest that you make plans to attend commencement just as other parents do. Don't ask or tell her. Just come. You want to see your daughter graduate.

Sincerely,

W. S.

We Live and Die—for What?

DEAR MRS. RIVERS,

What can I say?

Your husband's death is a great shock. He died confident that he was defending his country from communism, and he would not have had it any other way. As you know, he and I did not agree on a number of issues, but I respect his loyalty to what he believed was right.

I am sorry you have not heard from Hope, despite your letter and efforts to reach her by phone. You ask how she has received the news of her father's death. The answer is not comforting, I'm afraid. She says that she and her father had nothing in common, that she remembers nothing about him except the beatings he gave her when she was a little girl. But she said, "I don't hate him or his memory. When I heard about him, I didn't feel anything. I don't feel anything now. It's as if a stranger had died, somebody I didn't know and never met."

Hope still practices transcendental meditation twice each day. I am convinced that she is getting her kicks this way rather than by any mind-expanding drugs. The other day she said proudly, "I haven't had one joint of pot since following the beautiful Maharishi." I believe her.

Again I say, please accept my deepest sympathy in the loss of your husband, and may you be guided, comforted, and strengthened by a Presence greater than our own.

Sincerely,
W. S.

A Little Thing Called "Black"

DEAR MRS. RIVERS,

The transcendental meditation lasted exactly six weeks. Hope says it was a phase or a fad but she would not have missed it for anything.

She and her new boyfriend came by the office yesterday, and I must confess I did not recognize her. Her blue jeans were gone, shoes were on her feet, and her blond hair was shoulder length. She was wearing a dress—the first time in four years that I have seen Hope in a dress! Her face was scrubbed; she was radiant and looked every inch the sweetheart of the campus.

I am still in a state of shock. Hope is a magnificently beautiful girl, with a young Grace Kelly face and figure. How could she have mistreated herself as she has during these past several years? Her sarcasm and cynicism have disappeared; she is bright and gay, a transformation the likes of which I have never seen.

She came by not only to introduce me to her new boyfriend but to make a request of me (the only time she has ever asked me to do anything). Since she never communicates with you, she wanted me to write a letter to tell you about her boyfriend, the man she intends to marry the week before (not after) graduation. I told her I would be glad to undertake it.

This was perhaps an overstatement, for I am truly sorry, after the blow of your husband's death, to be so soon the bearer of other news which will, I'm afraid, be something of a shock to you. The young man to whom Hope is engaged is a Negro, a senior by the name of Frank Elder. His home is in Baltimore and his father is a prominent physician. He will enter Yale Medical School this fall. He and Hope already have an apartment in New Haven and will go there immediately after graduation. I have seen Frank around campus on a number of occasions. He does not participate in any campus or community activities—is arrogant and overbearing and has an intense contempt for white people. He is not a member of the campus chapter of the "Black Cats" but shares their views on black supremacy. He does not want to become identified with the "Cats" because they, too, are beneath him. He is a good deal of a loner and apparently revels in being upper-middle class.

It did not take me long to discover who the boss will be in the new Elder home. Frank will dominate and control Hope in marriage even as he has during their short engagement. When he says, "Put on shoes," she puts them on; when he says "Take a bath," she takes a bath; when he says, "Take those blue jeans off and put on a dress," she puts on a dress. If Hope was looking for a man who would discipline her, as she was disciplined in her early childhood, she has found him. Frank has plenty of money; he is tall, handsome, and ebony black (not tan)—carries himself like a Brahmin prince.

I asked him what he had against white people, the good and bad, the bigot and the nonbigot. He looked at me with contempt and said, "You're really asking why I dislike you, a so-called friend of the black man. I want nothing to do with you.

You're a liberal who would probably die of a stroke if your daughter ever wanted to marry a Negro." I protested to no avail.

I then asked Hope why they were getting married before graduation rather than after. Her reply was that all exams will be over and she and Frank can have a wonderful week together then. Also, she said with a twinkle in her eye, the marriage would prevent you from attending either the wedding or commencement. Hope thinks she knows how you will receive this announcement.

They will be married on a weekend in the latter part of May, in an Episcopal church (predominantly Negro) located in the ghetto not far from the campus. Frank is an Episcopalian.

Hope has gone through many fads and phases. I believe this one is for real.

Sincerely,
W. S.

A Big "If"

Dear Mrs. Rivers,

You write that you will attend neither the wedding nor commencement. Of course, this must be your own decision, but I shall be sorry if you stay away. Deep down in her heart, I think Hope would like you to be present at both ceremonies. I know she has tried to convey the opposite impression, but that attitude is a cover-up.

Unknown to Hope, Frank came by to see me this morning. He is puzzled by certain traumatic changes which have taken place in his own life. He said with acid in his voice, "I started going with Hope several months ago because I found her very available. It was *that* and nothing else. But since we've known each other her life has changed, and so has mine. I really have come to love her with my whole being. She is soul to me and I couldn't live without her. She's too good to be true."

He has been hung up on hating *all* white people, because if there were just one decent white person in the world there might be others. He is caught in the trap of his own suspicions. Sitting opposite me, he lowered his eyes and said, "We want you to come to the wedding. Hope's father is dead—will you take his place and give her away?"

I shall be there, and I trust you will be, too.

Sincerely,
W. S.

Give Them a Chance

DEAR MRS. RIVERS,

I am sorry you failed to show for either Hope's wedding or commencement. Time will change things, and I predict that one day you and she will develop a meaningful relationship.

I acted as her father and gave her away. They were married early Saturday afternoon in the small chapel of the Episcopal church. Aside from Hope and myself the only other white person present was my wife, who served as matron of honor. No others had been invited.

Dr. and Mrs. Elder were present. Frank's older brother, Dr. Josiah Elder, a brain surgeon, was best man. A number of Frank's Baltimore friends were there, but no Kingston students. Hope was lovely in a white, street-length dress with a short veil. She carried no flowers, only a white prayer book.

The wedding was impressive. Father Robert Goodwin, the rector (as black as Frank), conducted the service. He has a full, rich voice; when he asks the age-old questions, you have the feeling he means them. Hope says she is joining the Episcopal Church as soon as possible and that their children will be reared as strict Episcopalians. They have already found a church in New Haven, predominantly Negro, where they hope to become members. This is what Frank wants, and whatever Frank wants makes her happy.

Hope and Frank were a most striking pair at commencement. She fair and honey-blond, he ebony black, and both graceful, handsome, and aloof—they seemed oblivious to everyone around them. They appear to be lost in each other's love. I believe they'll make it *if* society gives them a chance.

I write to give you their new address: 8415 Ridgewood Avenue, Apt 16, New Haven, Connecticut.

Mrs. Rivers, my final word to you is: Find it in your heart to make the first move. There is still time. You may be surprised at the response you will receive.

Sincerely,

W. S.

III

To Mrs. Quinn,
concerning her daughter Bertha

Away from Home the First Time

DEAR MRS. QUINN,

You say it has been more than a week since you heard from Bertha.

In my judgment, your daughter does better at writing than any student I know. She is a sweet, conscientious girl who does what is exected of her and gives no one any trouble. She comes to chapel every Sunday and is active in the Religious Association. I checked with the band director and he says Bertha is doing well. She will never be a spectacular tuba player, but she practices long and hard, and he says she will improve. She never misses a rehearsal.

If I were you I would not worry too much about Bertha. She is only a sophomore, but in these two years she has made a number of friends, both boys and girls. She dates a different boy now and then. Bertha has her feet on the ground and does not permit little things to annoy or upset her. She doesn't seem to fret when she doesn't have a date for a dance; and she does not appear overly excited when a boy asks her out. She gives the impression that there is plenty of time ahead for her to do all the things she wants to do. Right now she is at Kingston to get an education and is determined to learn all she can.

Your telephone calls, two and three times a week, have become something of an embarrassment to her. Why not limit them to one a month? I realize that, along with thousands of parents, you are anxious about your only child, for whom the college years are her first experience away from home. But it seems to me you have less cause to worry than any parent I know.

Sincerely,

W. S.

This Is a Normal Campus

DEAR MRS. QUINN,

It is good to know that you have reduced the telephone calls to Bertha to one a week—one a month would be better, but this helps and will have to do.

In answer to your urgent question about a "sex orgy" at Kingston, it seems a pity to lose sleep, as you say you have been doing ever since, over a newspaper exaggeration. There are two things I can say.

a. It was misleading for the newspapers to label the incident as a "sex orgy." True, three Kingston couples left the campus last Saturday night and rented rooms under assumed names in a nearby motel. That they had sex I do not doubt, but this was not what caused them to be arrested. In this state, beer cannot be consumed by anyone until he is twenty-one. All these students were eighteen and nineteen, and all were drinking beer.

b. Bertha was not one of them. Names of the girls were not released to the press, but one of the descriptions, I realize, somewhat fitted Bertha: overweight, horn-rimmed glasses, bleached hair, etc. But I can substantiate what Bertha told you on the phone without any equivocation. *She was not one of them.* That night she was in the chapel rehearsing a part in a playlet that the Religious Association is giving next Sunday.

I have deep sympathy for your anxiety, but believe me, Kingston is quite a normal place. The things you read in the press often give the impression that this is a den of iniquity, but I assure you it is not. In fact, it is much quieter here than on most college campuses. It is unfortunate that occasionally an incident occurs, such as that of last Saturday night, which the newspapers like to play up. It is too bad that the good things of Kingston are not so fully reported.

Sincerely,

W. S.

The Study of Our Navels

DEAR MRS. QUINN,

Bertha does not even know Sue Blanton. I have checked this out. She does not know her, has no classes with her, and has never been on a date with her; the two girls have never even spoken to each other.

Sue Blanton is not the "girl of the streets" you picture her to be. She is a strong, independent young woman who, when she sees something she believes is wrong, tries to right it. "No decent human being would be opposed to compulsory chapel," you write. But I hope I am a decent human being and I am opposed to compulsory chapel. I have been opposed to it ever since I came here a number of years ago. Yet I did nothing about it. Sue Blanton and a number of her friends confronted the administration and the Board of Trustees, and compulsory chapel was eliminated. I accept as valid her trenchant comment: "No state, no institution, can force a person to worship God."

You were also aghast when you heard about the controversy concerning the use of rooms in the girls' dorms. Some of the girls, including Sue Blanton, felt that the college was discriminating against women—that women should have the same right to the use of their rooms as do men. You are correct as to the hours in which women can entertain men in their rooms—and believe me, the world is not coming to an end, and the reputation of Kingston as "a college with religious traditions" will not be ruined.

I happen to know that Bertha was *against* compulsory chapel and was *for* the "open" policy in the use of rooms in the girls' dorms. But Bertha is like the vast majority of Americans. We are *against* something or *for* something, but aside from sounding off with our tongues we never do anything. Sometimes I think our chapel programs are a deadening influence. Students attend, read, talk, and intellectualize, but they never act in the world. They feel that by singing, talking, praying, and appraising that they have done something, when in actuality they have *done* nothing. Sue Blanton knows the danger in group introspection (the study of our navels); therefore, once she has a conviction she acts upon it.

I wish Bertha and her chapel friends would talk less and act more. I can assure you—and I know it will be a relief to you—that Bertha and Sue are not friends. They do not know each other.

Sincerely,
W. S.

No Place to Hide

Dear Mrs. Quinn,

If you took Bertha out of Kingston and transferred her to another college, where would it be? State? Smith? Bennington—Radcliffe—Vassar—Barnard—N.Y.U.—? Aside from several colleges which are only borderline-accredited, the situation on each campus is quite similar.

These are days of ferment and excitement, of student upheaval and involvement. Changes in laws, customs, and rules and regulations are in the making—I, for one, welcome much of what is happening. At least I prefer this to the climate of a few years ago, when college students were interested and concerned about nothing except what to wear to the prom or the make of the latest foreign car.

Bertha came by my office last week and we had a long chat. She loves Kingston and her friends think highly of her. She is active in the chapel and is now in the varsity band. In just a few months she will be a senior. What a memorable time this last year of college can be! This is the only occasion when I have ever seen Bertha upset. Tears were in her eyes when she said, "I love it here. Can't you do something to persuade Mother to let me graduate with my class?"

As you have often pointed out, she has a serious weight problem. If you do not transfer her, she vows that in return she will lose twenty-five pounds. I think she means it.

I know you are distressed because of several things that have happened at Kingston; I realize Bertha is an only child and you are a widow; I know you worry about her—when she dates, and when she does not date. But please think long and hard before transferring her to another school. She is jolly and good-natured, she is doing academically acceptable work, she has a wholesome attitude toward college life and still plans to teach school upon graduation. In my judgment she is a good and dependable girl.

Think it over.

Sincerely,
W. S.

The Obedient One

DEAR MRS. QUINN,

I hardly know how to answer your letter of gratitude for the little I did for Bertha while she was an undergraduate.

Your decision to permit her to finish with her class was the right one—this I do not doubt. She was thrilled beyond words and has been more than keeping her promise to you ("I'll do anything Mother says if only she will let me stay"). For all I know she may have already fulfilled it to the letter and lost the twenty-five pounds! At least she is well on the way.

She certainly appears enthusiastic about her teaching. I understand George will get his Ph.D. in three more years. He is an excellent student and I know you are proud to have such a fine new son. I agree that it is better for him to stick to his classes and seminars and writing his thesis until he completes all the requirements. Many men spread out the Ph.D. work over such a long period that they are not only exhausted but practically old men when at last they are "doctored." Bertha is eager and willing to teach as long as it takes George to complete his work. After that, she says, she wants a dozen children.

I was deeply moved when she wrote to say that she wanted to be married in the Kingston chapel, with myself officiating at the ceremony. It was a pleasure and an honor.

I have never known a student who enjoyed her four years of college more than Bertha. Please do not thank me—it was not I who stood fast during the college years, it was your daughter.

Sincerely,

W. S.

IV
To Mrs. Van Brock,
concerning her son Mel

Mother's Love Is Great, But—

DEAR MRS. VAN BROCK,

You ask me what I think of your moving to Kingston. In my judgment there are several reasons why such a move would not be wise at this particular time. Mel is beginning his senior year; he has made an enviable record, but he needs more than ever to be on his own. Certainly he must feel that he can make it by himself.

As you know, seniors are permitted to live off campus. He may not have told you, but I am certain he does not mind if I give you this information. At the beginning of the new school year, about two weeks ago, he found a beautiful apartment two miles from the college. By car he is not more than ten minutes from any class. His roommate is a student by the name of Dave Bronston.

He never discusses his father's death—it may be a subject too sensitive for him. He often mentions you, and there is the usual ambivalence in his comments. However, I am quite sure he loves you and in every way has great respect for you. But at this stage of his life he would prefer that you live in Boston and he in Kingston. Under these circumstances you can see each other three or four times during the year, and then of course there are the holidays. On second thought, the coming Christmas holidays and spring vacation may be out, for Mel tells me that he and Dave Bronston are going to Bermuda for Christmas and to the Giant Hump ski resort for the spring break. But except for these times, you can visit him here whenever you like.

His senior recital will be sometime prior to the Christmas recess. I am sure he would enjoy having you come for that. Mel is by far the most accomplished music major at Kingston, and it is good news that he has already been accepted at Juilliard for graduate work.

Your question concerning his relation to other students is easily answered. Yes, he is liked by a large number of students, both men and women. Of course, one who has money in abundance never knows how much his popularity is due to being able to pick up the tab. But I get the impression that the students genuinely like Mel. Why shouldn't they? He is bright, handsome, and always appears to have a good word for everybody. In an academic community such as Kingston, most people are highly opinionated—often without justification. They are also sensitive, and critical of each other. If you do not hold the same political, religious, or social views, in some circles you are anathema. I suppose this is true on all college campuses. But Mel somehow finds it easy not to say the destructive word, but to find the right and helpful one. So you can see why he is so well liked. I enjoy having him come by the office. When I'm depressed—which these days does happen now and then—he's a joy to have around. He counsels me, "Chaplain, stay with it!" "We need you around here." "You're the one link between the administration and the students." So you see why I am fond of your son!

I can understand his unwillingness to write you as often as you think he should. Of course you want to know what he is doing, how he is getting along, who his friends are, and so on. But this lack of letter writing is characteristic of most students, especially men. The boys often do not write home more than once a semester—unless they need money. Of course, that does not apply to Mel.

To answer your repeated question— Though he dates little, Mel appears to enjoy the company of a number of girls, especially if they share his interest in music. His record collection of the classics is the largest in this area. To a certain extent this obsession with music applies to his men friends, virtually all of whom are music majors. That is, all except Dave Bronston. Dave is on the wrestling team, is not a good student, and gives me the impression that he is one friend Mel could do without. He is a "hanger-on," something of a sponger, and currently on academic probation.

Please believe me when I say I know how lonely you must have been since Mr. Van Brock's death. Mel, being an only child, is naturally the focal point of your love and concern. But as I said before, I urge you to reconsider your plan to move to Kingston for Mel's last year. Your son, having left the fraternity house, is happier than I have ever seen him. He is on his own, he goes and comes as he pleases, and he lives a life that most students (and most people) in this country envy.

You ask about his meals. As you know, he is not a hearty eater but likes unusual and special foods. Somewhere he has picked up an amazing knowledge of French cooking! My wife and I were his first guests in the new apartment last week. He gave us *sole amandine* and a delicious Chablis—it was awfully good. Though he now drinks only moderately—very little, to be exact—he knows wines, the best French and Italian. It was quite an experience for us to see his new place and enjoy his hospitality.

I know he will always be to you "my little boy." But he is twenty-two years old—nearly twenty-three. He has struggled to become a real person and in my judgment he has made it.

Trusting to see you at Mel's recital, I am

Sincerely yours,

W. S.

We Do Not Dig Each Other

DEAR MRS. VAN BROCK,

Well now! Mel's recital was a spectacular success. The reporter who covered it is a piano major and has done some work at Juilliard. Her review, as you have no doubt read, was ecstatic; everyone was thrilled beyond words.

I was interested to hear that you attended chapel service last Sunday, conducted by my assistant, Chaplian Croy. Your inquiry is noted—I also detect in your letter more than a hint of hostility to him.

Chaplain Croy has been my assistant for about two years. He is married, has a new baby, and is a graduate of Union Theological Seminary in New York. He is of the younger breed of clergymen, and though I do not always agree with his views, language, dress, habits, or programs, I find him interesting and exciting Perhaps there is a generation gap among the clergy. My being unable fully to understand him or "get with him" is an illustration of it.

With long hair, a black beard, and strong speech he might well be the prophet Hosea brought to life. His language is sprinkled with the cuss words of the day plus all the terms and phrases common to the hippie. His street clothes, which you did not see, are Nehru jackets decorated with love beads or peace medallions. The life of love is his theme song.

Twice a month he is responsible for the morning service in chapel. No one can predict what he will do or what to expect in the service. He is strong on the interpretative dance (which you saw), far-out dramas, and jazz. Unlike myself, he minimizes the sermon and often replaces it with a folk singer playing a guitar and singing protest songs. He spends considerable time in the local pool hall and bars, and he insists that Jesus, if he were here today, would be in the pool hall and bars rather than in church. According to Chaplain Croy, Jesus would find most church services unbearable.

But note this, Mrs. Van Brock: he reaches a type of student that I could never reach. He is a religious man, but is not considered by most students to be a part of the "religious establishment." He is with them and not "one of us." In all candor I tell you the following which concerns Mel. At the beginning of the school session last year, Mel returned to campus in a rebellious, angry mood. He was angry with the government, angry with the college, but most of all he appeared to be angry with you. He started drinking heavily and was on the verge of throwing everything overboard, even his music. Chaplain Croy had just joined our staff. It was he who saved your son from disillusionment with life in the world and at Kingston. If you have anyone to thank for Mel's recovery of his old self, it is not I but Chaplain Croy. If you write further derogatory letters to Mel about Chaplain Croy, it will simply alienate you further from your son.

In the midst of his unusual ways, Chaplain Croy is a religious man. Every time I hear him pray in chapel I am deeply moved. I have copied excerpts from some of his prayers, and I enclose them.

O God, here are two seniors in love. They have been having sex together several times a week for two years. Help them to deepen their commitment so that each will fully contribute to the growth and maturity of the other.

Again,

O God, he has discovered that he is a homosexual. Help him to endure the shock, give him strength to accept his own condition and resist the temptation of self-hatred because of it. May he never force his attentions on anyone, young or old, but permit only those relationships which will further the well-being of himself and others.

Again,

O God, he is black, she is white and they are married. As society seeks to destroy them, may their love for each other grow. Bless their children and help them to meet without inner damage the insanities of our day.

Again,

O God, our trouble is we do not dig each other. We play at communication and understanding. Break our pride, bury our hostility, destroy our suspicion, until in love we learn to touch each other, speak to each other, and accept each other.

Again,

O God, father of Jesus, I need you! Today I incinerated a Zantusi village of old men and women, young mothers and their children. Can I ever atone for this? There is nothing I can do to cleanse myself or to relieve the bloodstain. Accept my cry of hate—I hate myself, I hate the country which demands this of me—I hate, I hate, I hate.

Again,

O God, some of us are hooked on pot, not because it is so great but because we have found our kicks here rather than in your Kingdom. Nothing reveals our emptiness, our nakedness, more than this. A corrupt society is waiting to be destroyed, a floundering, unyielding government dares to be challenged, a helpless, dying world waits for someone who cares. Help us to find our kicks where it counts—before it is too late.

Not only are his prayers marked by a deep sincerity, but he offers his friendship to students with no questions asked. They do not have to explain, defend, or justify themselves. If they are on narcotics, he will not preach to them; he seeks to show them a better way. If they are baffled and angered by the draft he identifies with them. He recognizes the positive role which sex can play in their personal lives, but when sex becomes a cheap, mean, exploitive experience, he debates with them long into the night—and he is an articulate debater.

All of us here at Kingston are grateful for your generous gifts in the past, and needless to say we hope you will see fit to honor and assist us again.

Both Chaplain Croy and I are eager to effect a more understanding relation between you and Mel. We shall do everything possible to accomplish this.

Sincerely yours,
W. S.

An Open and Honest Discussion

DEAR MRS. VAN BROCK,

It was nice to have you on campus last week, though your appearance was somewhat of a surprise, not only to me but also to Mel.

The incident three days after your visit will not interfere with Mel's scholastic standing or his graduation. It will not likely alienate him from either students or faculty. We are living in a new day; it may not be a better day, but it is a new one. The situation Mel finds himself in is now being understood and accepted by a growing segment of our society.

It is true that Mel served as chairman of the committee which sponsored the meeting to consider the status of homosexuals in our society and on campus. A young woman, a lesbian, from Boston and a graduate student, homosexual, from Greenwich Village, spoke. There were approximately two hundred people present. There were no harangues, no threats, brawls, riots, or other disturbances. Each guest spoke for about forty minutes, following which there was a question-and-answer period. I am glad I attended the meeting (it was open to the public). It was civilized as well as educational.

The speakers stressed four points: First, homosexuality has a long history: Socrates and many of the Caesars, David and Jonathan, Jesus and John. (I debated the latter point during the question-and-answer time but the speakers stuck to their guns.) They insisted that many of our greatest poets, musicians, writers, and statesmen have been of the "other sex." Of course, even a slight knowledge of history confirms this.

Second, homosexuality is not something the homosexual chooses. He may be active or inactive, overt or nonovert, but his nature has been determined by early circumstances and experiences over which he had no control.

The speakers differed on two points: the first concerned the bi-sexual nature of all people. The lesbian insisted that all people are homosexual some of the time and that no one is homosexual all the time. The male speaker would not accept this, simply because he had discovered by personal experience that the basic nature of certain people, especially adults, tended toward total "maleness" or total "femaleness."

The second point of difference was in the use of the term "sexuality." The lesbian often used it in a broader sense, so that at times the term could have been a synonym for the thrust for life. The homosexual more narrowly restricted the use of the term to what we ordinarily refer to as sexual activity or interest.

The differences at these two points made an interesting exchange.

Third, each said in a different way that, in a society struggling to be free, there must be free sexual practices among consenting adults. Sex is such a personal, private matter that laws which seek to control or punish those who participate in it succeed only in driving sex underground or of robbing it of its joy.

They further pointed out that responsible homosexuals abhor forced relations, and in this regard they would be in favor of strong laws, federal or state. *These would apply equally to all persons who force themselves on another.* I was interested that the speakers included "persuasion" as a means of force. Where force or persuasion of children is involved, the responsible homosexual would be in favor of extended jail terms and treatment until the violator can safely live in freedom.

Fourth, society is becoming somewhat more tolerant of those whose nature is unlike that of the majority. The subject is now discussed on radio and television, and treated on the stage and in movies. More people are aware of other people unlike themselves, and this has created a degree of tolerance in certain areas. However—and here the speakers made their strongest point of the evening—the major problem is in the homosexual's acceptance of himself. How does he see himself? How does he interpret himself? Can he accept himself? If he rejects himself he plunges into a psychological jam—hating and repelled by his own inclinations and desires. In anxiety he alternates between self-hate and maudlin self-pity; he sometimes tries to make himself believe that his condition is not for real and that he can by strength and will power, or sometimes by prayer and meditation, effectively change it. This is often the way of misery and unhappiness.

On the other hand, he can often with the aid of professional help, come to grips with the situation and finally, in a moment of truth, accept himself. Having done so, he is free either to work with his counselor toward a transformation into the heterosexual pattern or to accept the singularity of his nature, and strive to live in society as normally as possible. This latter path is a difficult one because the bulk of society (though changing in its interpretation) has not accepted him. He knows that on the books are various laws which seek to control and deny him the real expression of his nature. Thus a furtive life of secrecy must characterize his daily existence. This is especially true as it applies to holding a job or keeping an apartment. But the important point for the homosexual—he has accepted himself.

Mel has found Kingston to be a fairly accepting place. For all its faults and shortcomings, maniacal persecution of the responsible homosexual is not one of them. Our community on campus appears to say, "Live and let live." This is not the attitude of trustees and alumni who read about the open meeting for homosexuals in various papers—it made the AP. The administration is being criticized for permitting the meeting to be held, but Dean Blower is sticking by his decision, and I predict he will weather the storm.

In closing, I must say our legislators recently revealed a condition of near idiocy in the matter of law-making. Strong gun laws—registration, licensing, and confiscation—cannot be passed; thus, in this country we shall continue to kill six thousand people each year with guns (60,000 in ten years!). But the same legislators do not hesitate to pass strict laws regulating the act of sex, even detailing what can and cannot be performed in a bedroom by properly married couples!

I close by saying that Mel is a candidate for the presidency of the senior class. The election will be held next month, and I predict he will win.

Sincerely,

W. S.

On Being "Like That"

Dear Mrs. Van Brock,

This is to say how very sorry I am that you have found it necessary to enter a sanatorium. I hope and pray that your confinement will not be lengthy. I know Dr. Gustav Miger personally and consider him one of the outstanding psychiatrists in the country. On more than one occasion I have recommended students, members of the faculty, and parents to him. He seems to have the magic touch.

Mel has accepted his condition, but you insist that you have not accepted it and never will. His being "like that" is bad enough, you say, but to parade it in public where your friends could read about it is too much. I sympathize with your position, and at this stage of my life I wonder if my reaction as a parent would be any different. I can intellectualize the problem of the homosexual, but I have emotional difficulty in accepting him. To those of us who have enjoyed a "normal" sex life, the way of the "pervert" is too much—he is strange, he is unclean.

The thing I am working on now as far as my own perspective is concerned is to understand that physical equipment alone does not make a man a man or a woman a woman. He may have a penis, but this does not make him a man; she may have breasts and a vagina, but this does not make her a woman. The thing that determines maleness and femaleness is one's basic nature; it is thoughts, desires, imagination, feelings, and responses. Thus, it is possible for a "man" to have the nature of a woman, and for a "woman" to have the nature of a man. This may be due to heredity—which few psychologists accept—or it may be due to certain environmental influences which prevailed in early life. As you probably know, some authorities place great emphasis on the relationship between the male child and his mother. I do not know how much weight to attach to this, except to say that in several cases with which I have worked it appears to have been a factor.

You lament the idea that Mel may never marry, that he will never give you grandchildren. If, in truth, Mel is strongly homo-sexual, it would be far better that he never marry. For such a man to marry a "normal" woman is to subject her to every sort of frustration and indignity. He is detached, aloof, and unre-sponsive. Her "femaleness" is distasteful to him. He does not respond to her physical allure or to her pleas. He cannot endure to sleep with her or touch her in any way, other than by a platonic caress. If such a man is in some form of public life, it is often to his advantage to have a wife and even more to have children. He will force himself to have relations with his wife for the sole purpose of getting her pregnant—procreation. Once conception has taken place, he leaves her to live with her own unfulfilled desires. If Mel is "like that," I hope he will never marry.

Mel and Dave Bronston are no longer living together. Dave left school, has been drafted, and is now out of the country. As far as Mel is concerned that relationship is over. However, he has a new roommate—Joe Mendes, a senior who is also a music major. Though I never liked Dave, I approve of Joe. He is a clean-cut young man but quite serious. He does not possess Mel's friendly, outgoing, and charming manner, but he is solid and responsible.

Senior class elections were held yesterday. Mel was elected president by an overwhelming vote. It appears that he has not only accepted himself, but his classmates have accepted him! Now it is up to you. I offer the suggestion that as soon as you can work through the problem, as soon as you can find it in your heart to accept your son all the way, you will be on the road to recovery.

Sincerely,

W. S.

Some Turn the Corner and Some Do Not

DEAR MRS. VAN BROCK,

Your last letter is more coherent and less self-pitying; I can only assume from this that you are well on your way to recovery.

You indicate that Dr. Miger has explained Mel's condition in terms similar to those which I recently set forth, and also says that you are not likely to recover your health until there is a genuine acceptance of Mel and his present condition.

Now, as to your question whether I agree with the psychiatrist that there is little chance that Mel will ever change—that he can be cured. Of course, my knowledge and experience are limited compared to those of a practicing psychiatrist. However, I would agree substantially with your doctor. It is possible that Mel may never change or be completely "cured." A lad of ten, eleven, twelve is naturally attracted to boys his own age. He prefers their companionship to that of girls. During this time there may be some sort of limited sex play between boys. But at the magic age of fifteen, sixteen, and seventeen boys turn their attention to girls. They still like each other and enjoy each other in games such as baseball, basketball, football, and so forth, but their thoughts are apt to be obsessed with girls. In most instances the obsession is sexual. Boys are sometimes gratified just by looking and talking with girls, or even smelling them, but most of all they crave to fondle and touch them. By the time they are nineteen or so, they reach the greatest level of sexual interest and capacity. Sexual outlets and abilities at this age are fantastically high, and in this connection, I insist, these young men are objects of envy to older males long past their prime. Many harsh and bitter attitudes of older men toward the younger are rooted in this well-known psychological condition. Elderly men still have fiery thoughts and desires but lack the capacity or the opportunity to fulfill them! It is no accident that all secular and ecclesiastical repressive sexual measures are instigated by middle-aged and older men.

Mrs. Van Brock, there are some boys who, for a variety of psychological reasons, do not turn the corner. Girls are not for them a source of interest, nor are they sexually aroused by them. Their interests and attachments are still with boys. As this condition continues into adulthood, the twig is bent, the basic nature is formed, and the likelihood of its ever turning back or being redirected is slight indeed. For such people the life of shame, torment, and furtiveness begins. Society brands them "unclean" as the lepers of old; they are considered perverted. Harsh laws are passed, not simply to control forcible contacts, but to prohibit voluntary acts by consenting adults.

I trust that your acceptance of Mel will produce helpful changes in your own life and will make a positive contribution to him in his difficult situation.

Sincerely,

W. S.

The Joys of Separation

DEAR MRS. VAN BROCK,

In the very near future, the President and Dean Blower will be writing you their words of gratitude for your magnificent gift to the college. As a result of my close relationship with Mel during these past four years, and my correspondence with you, I feel that I know you as a friend. So at this time I want to express my personal appreciation for what you have done for the college.

It is appropriate that the new building should be called the "Van Brock Theater and Music Hall." I understand it is to be located on the slope of the hill fronting the lake, the loveliest spot on campus. This will give Kingston the most complete theatrical building complex of any college in the East. Today's students are taking an increased interest in the theater and this pleases me a great deal. Serious dramatists of yesterday, both in Europe and this country, said something significant about the condition of man and the meaning of life. It is likely that we are on the threshold of a new era. After a drought of several years, contemporary dramatists will begin to make their influence felt, and they too will have something significant to say about the world in which we live.

Also, the music department will be pleased to have its own building immediately adjacent to the new theater! It is wonderful to think of the air-conditioned classrooms, offices, rehearsal rooms, and the beautiful hall for recitals and other musical presentations. I know Mel is pleased about this.

Speaking of Mel—it was a surprise to learn that he has postponed his enrollment at Juilliard. In accepting the invitation from the Soviet government to study at the conservatory in Moscow, he says he will realize a lifelong ambition. As you know, Russian has been his language major at Kingston for four years. His facility in writing and speaking the language will add immensely to enjoyment of the Soviet venture. He is impressed with the emphasis the Russians place on the classics, especially in music and more especially in piano. A piano concert in Moscow, he says, creates as much excitement and attracts as many people as a boxing match, football game, or an Audrey Hepburn movie in this country. Mel says that by the time he returns he believes the tide will have turned in the States so that concert music will be in demand on radio, television, and on the stage. For this day we can pray!

I understand he plans to leave for the Soviet Union immediately after commencement. The two of you will not have long to visit. However, I hope you will have time to say those necessary things related to a better understanding of each other.

You asked me a direct question, "How does Mel feel about me now?"

I can only say that he has great respect for you and in his way he loves you. You have almost convinced him that you no longer consider him "unclean." You accept him as he is. These two or three years when Mel is out of the country will be good for both of you. He will have time to think through his problems, and with your improved health you will be able to grow in appreciation of a wonderful son.

Yes, Mel wants you to come to commencement. Of this I am sure. Until then, I am

Sincerely,

W. S.

V
To Mrs. Soper
concerning her daughter Mary Ann

Beauty and Background

Dear Mrs. Soper,

At this time I cannot with confidence evaluate your daughter's problem. She may be in need of psychiatric attention, and then again she may not. A little more time will tell. You will be pleased to know that Mary Ann is academically still first in the sophomore class. If she continues on this level there is certainly no danger of her losing the scholarship and loan.

I am sorry to hear that your husband's condition is worse and that it is necessary for you to work overtime to keep the family together. Mary Ann told me about her younger sisters—eight and nine, I believe—and how much help they are around the house and with Mr. Soper. You and your husband must be superior people to have reared three girls of such high caliber.

You indicate that your sister will remain with you to help care for your husband until the first of the year, but that she is leaving then to be married. However, I suggest that for the coming year you try to find a nursing home for your husband. Some sort of care will be imperative, since you will be working. Practical nurses are almost impossible to find, and the financial burden would be too great in any case. Could you perhaps begin now to investigate the government's program relating to nursing homes? It is good to know that your husband will shortly receive permanent disability assistance through Social Security. The payments, though small, should help, and I hope they will come through without delay.

Part of Mary Ann's problem is rooted in her lack of confidence in herself. It is difficult to understand how anyone first in her class at Kingston (where academic standards are exceptionally high) could feel inadequate. Though she is rather shy, especially with strangers, I have noticed a warmth and responsiveness once you get to know her. There is really no reason for her to feel inferior.

You say she stopped writing when you could not afford to buy her the contact lenses. I asked her about this, and she said it was a disappointment but that she understood the family's financial plight. Nevertheless, she has had to face the fact that she is not beautiful. She is now resigned to the idea that contact lenses would not really have helped her face or form. I reminded her that her situation does not differ from that of the vast majority of young girls in this country who possess neither a beautiful face nor a gorgeous figure. But Mary Ann insisted it was not the contact lenses that caused her to withdraw further into her shell.

Then, amid anguish and tears, it came out. More than anything in the world she wanted to be pledged to Delta Mu Delta. (Or any sorority, for that matter.) Her strong academic record recommended her for consideration, but she was blackballed, the reason being that her "background" was not sufficiently strong to make the sorority accept her. My lack of sympathy for this whole sorority-fraternity system would be hard to exaggerate. It is superficial, undemocratic, and cruel. It has no place in American life—it is senseless exclusiveness. Please, Mrs. Soper, do not worry about this. Mary Ann will handle it and be a stronger person because of it.

Also, try to forget about the contact lenses. She has already overcome this disappointment. Don't ride her too hard about writing. There is not much for her to write about. Her life at Kingston at the moment is heavy with monotony. I often wonder how she endures her present sense of isolation.

Please keep me informed about your husband's condition and also your decision concerning his future, come the first of the year.

Sincerely,
W. S.

Heavy Is the Lonely Heart

DEAR MRS. SOPER,

It is great news that your husband will not have to go into a nursing home. As you know, these traps for the aged, though necessary, are one of the most depressing aspects in American life. Even while making the suggestion, I couldn't help feeling that for a man as young as Mr. Soper it would be a double tragedy. Who knows? Perhaps the paralysis will improve enough so that he can be up and about and also do some of the household chores.

To answer your question. As far as I know Mary Ann still has made no friends. She is a very lonely girl. Shy and reserved, she unconsciously makes it hard for anyone to get acquainted with her. Her classmates she easily dismisses by saying that they are unfriendly. Most of her extra time is spent in her room or in the library with books. High marks are her chief satisfaction at Kingston. But she really needs friends, and she needs them now. Two different roommates have recently moved away from her. They found her irritable and moody. I have spoken to several sympathetic students in the girls' dorm, suggesting that they try in some way to make contact with her. But they say it is impossible. They also insist it is not girl friends she needs—it is boy friends.

You say she never had a date in high school—that she went to no proms, parties, or informal dances. Surely this is a pity. Yet Mary Ann's case is typical of a good many college young people. Dating is not easy, it is loaded with many barriers. A number of men students keep away from Mary Ann, not simply because she is not "good-looking" but because of her intellectual superiority. She is far in advance of her sophomore standing. Dating involves talk—it is mostly an exciting give-and-take of conversation. College men just out of their teens are easily threatened by a highly intelligent girl. The academic barrier appears to be the most difficult for students to bridge—harder than race, social standing, or money. And this is especially true when it is the girl who happens to be superior. It is the reason, I think, that so many junior and senior men rush freshman girls. They have at least two years of college work on their side, and it is harder for the younger girl to question or challenge them. Dating is a difficult, hazardous business to begin with. Some students date too much, many not at all; while a few have the knack of putting this activity in its proper place.

You ask about Mary Ann's faith. This is not an easy question to answer. It is obvious that she is interested in the works of Bonhoeffer and Tillich and has been strongly influenced by them. She appears to have a profound faith in God, a faith that is emotionally experienced and intellectually satisfying. She feels that one's religious interest should be more concerned with people than with God—that God is less concerned with what people think of Him than with what they think of each other. He could not care less, she feels, what people do for Him when they don't care about what they do to and for each other. Service to God is never detached from the service to people and their needs. So her faith appears to be real, but she has no interest in or respect for the "organized" or "institutional" church. As far as I can tell, she never attends chapel on campus or church in town.

Yet she believes in "the church." I asked her the other day what she felt the church is in the world to do. She said, "The church is not something we go to, the church is people who have found out, with God's help, how to understand and care for each other. Wherever there are people who care, there is the church." This is an interesting statement, especially from an isolated young person who is struggling to find ways of expressing her own concern.

Mary Ann then told me two stories which explain why, if she were going to have faith in the church, it had to be rooted in something other than an organization or institution. She pointed out that in 1632 Galileo was branded a heretic by the church for his statement that the planets revolve around a stable sun. In 1633 the church forced him to repudiate the statement to save his own life. Recently, the church announced that the case had been officially reopened—presumably for the purpose of absolving Galileo from the guilt of his assertion! This, Mary Ann feels, is what happens when the church is an organization or institution: it is concerned not with the needs of people but with forms, hierarchy, programs, and untenable doctrines.

The second story concerns a church building and a billboard. On Route 46 in New Jersey, near your home, Mary Ann says there is a fitting monument to the life of the church in the world. On the north side of the highway a large, beautiful church has been erected. It stands as a holy reminder to all passing by that here is where the God of goodness, truth, beauty —the God of love and justice—is to be worshiped and served. Just before reaching it, however, the east-going motorist is confronted by a huge sign advertising a miniature Disneyland. This billboard, which obscures the view of the church, reads IN THE LAND OF MAKE-BELIEVE. With its irrelevant pronouncements, its token concern for people, and its preoccupation with its own survival, the church is dwarfed by the billboard.

As a minister, I have pondered your daughter's description of the nature and mission of the church, and two thoughts remain with me. First, she may be right. The church must not be obsessed with perpetuating itself; it must discover how to express love and justice. Second, young people of today will never take seriously a church that tries to keep them moral and intellectual infants. They have thrown away their toys and broken out of the ecclesiastical kindergarten. The church, if it is to survive, must understand this.

I met Mary Ann in the Sweet Shoppe the other day and we had a soda. It was a good time for me to ask about her major and what she wants to do when she finishes Kingston. She would like very much to major in religion but is even more enthusiastic about psychology. She wants to enter graduate school and go for a Ph.D. in clinical psychology. She then hopes to work in a clinic or hospital with mentally and emotionally disturbed children. This ambition must not be denied!

As you can see, Mrs. Soper, I think highly of your daughter. In my judgment she has very great potential. Somehow, in some way, we must see to it that she realizes her hopes and dreams. She is a tremendous human being and I hope you are proud of her.

Please give my regards to your husband.

Sincerely,

W. S.

Getting Out of the Shell

DEAR MRS. SOPER,

Just a hurried note to say that Mary Ann came by the office today in a whirl of excitement. She could hardly contain herself. A group of students, juniors and seniors, are going to Giant Hump for four days of skiing at the semester break in the first part of February. One of the invited girls came down with flu and was forced to cancel out. Mary Ann's new roommate asked her to take the sick girl's place. There will be five men and five women in the group—the men will stand all the expenses. Mary Ann is overjoyed. The girls have accepted her and the young man she will date appears amiable. It should work out.

Mary Ann has never before skied, but neither have several of the other girls. Her roommate assures her she will have a glorious time even without skiing. The boys like nothing better than to teach the girls. This may be the beginning of something important: an opportunity for her to make friends with men and women, her contemporaries. They will leave Thursday and return Sunday night. Registration for the new term begins Monday.

Mary Ann appeared pleased when I told her I had written a friend of mine in psychology at Northwestern about the possibilities of getting her into graduate school. I explained to him that there would be financial difficulties. The professor replied that if the student in question was as good academically as I indicated, he felt sure there would be no difficulty in getting her accepted. Furthermore, he seemed to think that in addition to a generous scholarship, Mary Ann could work as a student instructor in his department. Since she is only a sophomore, we agreed to keep in touch and I promised to inform him periodically about her record and achievements.

Things are moving. Let's keep our fingers crossed.

Sincerely,

W. S.

Happiness Is a Thing Called "Acceptance"

DEAR MRS. SOPER,

It was difficult for me to speak frankly to you on the telephone last night, but I think you surmised the situation. Mary Ann is pregnant, a little more than two months. The incident occurred during the ski party at the semester break. Please don't panic. I regret that it is impossible for you to make the trip here, but you must certainly stay with your job. Mr. Soper and your little girls all need you.

As far as I am able, and with Mary Ann's permission, I will bring you up to date with the developments. First of all, in my stupidity I did not take you quite seriously when you said Mary Ann had never dated a boy. I just assumed it was an exaggerated statement. But I understand better now. She had never dated, never been kissed, and in no discernible way had she ever touched or been touched by a boy. In the midst of her academic achievements, sex was never a part of her education. Her pathetic cry to me was, "We did it only four times—how can you get pregnant so quickly?" I could hardly believe my ears. I'm not telling you this to make you feel you have failed as a parent. All of us—parents, church, school, college—have failed. In my judgment there are more young girls in this country like Mary Ann than there are sophisticated girls who know all the questions and all the answers.

She is frightened at the prospect of being pregnant, is deeply troubled at causing you further burden and anguish, and fears that this experience will destroy her chances of going to graduate school. However, she insists in the midst of her fears that those four days were the happiest of her college life—perhaps the only happy days. She was accepted by her group, the girls were gay and friendly, and the boy she dated seemed kind and sympathetic. After a lifetime of peer rejection and isolation, is it any wonder that she responded to this type of warmth and acceptance? She was accepted as a person, she was touched and loved by a man. She played in the sun and snow, and at night before a roaring fire the group gathered around the piano and sang. As is the custom in certain ski lodges, the boys and girls paired off and slept with each other. "I may never get to do it again, but for once in my life I was happy!" So spoke Mary Ann.

Her feet are now on the ground and she has come back to reality. The harsh unrealities of reality are ugly and difficult to bear. Society says that a woman must not have intercourse before marriage; society says, furthermore, that having a baby out of wedlock is the worst calamity that could befall any girl. She is ruined forever and her family has suffered the ultimate disgrace. Our customs will not tolerate the unwed mother or her child. Years ago I had a professor—of theology, no less—who often said, "A woman was born to bear children; the maternal instinct is denied only at great risk to health and happiness. A society which consigns a woman, unwed, to a childless existence is a cruel society; a society which condemns the woman, unwed, because she bears a child, is indeed a sick society." After dealing with a number of girls in this predicament, I am almost ready to agree with my favorite professor.

Practical fact demands that we accept what society says or be destroyed. Therefore secrecy in handling this situation must be maintained. We must organize as if we were in some deep conspiracy, and we must proceed rather hypocritically, as if a grievous sin against God had been committed as well as an act of violence against society. For the sake of Mary Ann and her baby, whatever we now decide to do must be done in absolute secrecy. In my next letter, which you will receive within a few days (after I have recovered my wits), I shall outline the various options before us.

I asked the young man who was Marry Ann's date and escort on the ski trip to come and see me and I explained the situation to him. I am at this time not permitted to give you his name. He is a junior, twenty years of age and at Kingston on a generous scholarship. He is not a good student and his scholarship is in jeopardy. His father operates a filling station in Hartford. The family have modest means and are strict members of a fundamentalist sect. The news of their son's involvement with a pregnant girl would destroy them. As with Mary Ann, no one in their family has ever graduated from college. They are proud of their son and counting on him to bring them status and recognition.

He is in a state of shock. He cannot believe that Mary Ann had never dated before, or that she could be so unaware of the "facts of life." He further cannot believe that a college girl would take such a trip unprepared. He found her not apprehensive or inclined to withdraw, but warm, eager, and responsive. He says with bitterness that he will marry her, quit school, and find a job. I asked him if he had any enduring feeling of love or affection for her and his reply was "No!" But he would marry her. What an unholy, ghastly business this is!

Mary Ann says that under no circumstances would she marry the boy. She is aware of his complete detachment; essentially they are total strangers. But unlike the boy, she feels no bitterness and little remorse for what has happened. Her one overwhelming reaction at this point is fear—fear of discovery; fear and apprehension for you, her father, her young sisters; and fear for the welfare of the child.

In this world, Mrs. Soper, one of the mysteries of life is not simply unequal privilege but unequal and undeserved suffering. It seems to me that you have had more than your share. When I see such things I think of the cross of Christ. His was a life of undeserved suffering. I admire your strength as well as your apparent understanding of this latest development.

I assure you I shall do whatever is in my power to save the lives of these two young people and to make your own burden easier.

Sincerely,
W. S.

Easy To Be Cruel

DEAR MRS. SOPER,

To set your mind at ease, let me say at once that Mary Ann appears equal to the demands of the present situation. She goes to class in a normal way and otherwise stays in her room with her books, much as she has always done. Quite often she comes by my office for a chat. As far as I know she has not seen the father of her child except at a distance. She simply says without bitterness, "We're really strangers." She will come through this experience and perhaps be a wiser and better person because of it.

Now for the options before us. First, marriage is out of the question. The young man, sullen and bitter, would quit school and marry her. She will have none of that.

Second, she could drop out of school, keep her baby, and return to live with you. For a variety of reasons, including your own precarious financial situation, your husband's health, as well as the emotional life of your two daughters, this does not seem feasible.

Third, she could have an abortion. It is not quite three months. We could find a doctor who would perform the operation at a minimum cost. If this appeared to be the path of wisdom, I would be more than glad to share the expense. But I do not believe that abortion is the answer. Nearly half a million young women in this country each year find themselves in Mary Ann's condition. A percentage of them (we are not sure exactly what it is) resort to abortion as the way out. Not all of them by any means have the operation in a back-alley boarding house or roadside motel. For those who can pay, abortions are performed by outstanding physicians under the safest possible conditions (and for a handsome fee). Studies reveal that, though many of these girls stand the operation physically, the emotional factors in being aborted are often harsh and lingering. I am against it, not on religious grounds (there are certain instances where it is the only way out) but because of the shock to the woman who undergoes the operation.

Putting these three options aside leaves us only one other: a good home for unwed mothers, where a high order of secrecy and professional attention will be maintained. Mary Ann can have the baby under the best supervision, put it out for adoption, and in due time return to Kingston to complete her education with not more than three or four people knowing what has taken place. No one among your friends or family, including your husband and your daughters, need ever know. Of course, the administration here must never know. If they did, her scholarship and loan would be withdrawn and she would be asked to leave. (Colleges, too, must play the cruelty game.)

Sensing that this last option was the only one open to us, I have, with Mary Ann's permission and approval, contacted a home in Ohio with which I am familiar. In recent years I have sent a number of our girls there. She will remain at Kingston until classes are over in the middle of May. At this time she will be a little more than three months pregnant and quite inconspicuous. She will go from here directly to the Ohio home. During the summer she will write a letter to Dean Blower explaining that due to her father's serious illness she will be forced to drop out of school for one semester, but that if all goes well she will reenroll next February. Several members of the administration know of Mr. Soper's illness; thus they are likely in this case to be considerate and compassionate.

The baby is due in October. Mary Ann will sign the necessary papers there, and adoption will be immediate. She will leave the Ohio home around the first of November and return, not to Kingston, but to your house. You must be ready with a believable story for your husband and daughters. She will remain with you through November, December, and January. Around the first of February, when the new semester begins, she will return to Kingston with no one the wiser, not even her roommate. We are involved in a grand conspiracy to save your daughter from a twisted society, shot through with its own measure of hypocrisy, and we must successfully pull it off!

Please do not worry about expenses. The home in Ohio is giving us reduced rates. The college has a Chaplain's Discretionary Fund, disbursed mainly for emergency bail for students who are jailed for picketing and demonstrating. I am sure some of the money can be used for this purpose with no questions asked.

Last week I made an appointment for Mary Ann, not with the college physician, but with our city's best gynecologist. I explained the situation to him. He will of course keep his mouth shut, and there will be no expense. Mary Ann will see him under an assumed name, even as she will be admitted to the Ohio home with an assumed name, an alias. The doctor's report from last week's visit indicates that she is in excellent health and that an easy delivery is expected. He said to me, "This girl is strong and healthy and she is big in the right places. She was born to have babies."

I think we have things pretty well squared away. If there are any questions, please feel free to write or call, collect—always, of course, with the discretion we have so far maintained. In the face of many difficulties you have been strong and understanding. Yours is a true profile in courage.

Sincerely yours,
W. S.

The Gift of the Cross

DEAR MRS. SOPER,

A lot of water has gone under the bridge during these past two years! Mary Ann has more than made it. Your family is proud of her, friends are proud of her, Kingston is proud of her —and more than anyone else, *I* am proud of her.

Let me thank you for the gift of the cross. You shouldn't have done that, but it is appreciated none the less. I shall hang it on the wall in my study at the chapel. When I look at it, I shall remember you, your patience and your strength.

I am delighted that Mr. Soper and your little girls will be able to come to commencement. It is a miracle that he has improved so much. I have arranged rooms for you at Mrs. Lane's house, a block from the campus. We will also have a wheel chair ready for your husband.

I know both of you are pleased beyond words at Mary Ann's

achievements. The semester of summer school, plus extra points in her regular schedule, have really done the trick and enabled her to graduate with flying colors as one of her class. Perhaps she has not told you—she is still so shy and modest about herself—but she is graduating not only a Phi Beta Kappa, but she is summa cum laude, number one in her class! She has had no difficulty getting into graduate school; in fact, eight or ten schools, on the basis of her record here, have contacted her. But she will be going to Northwestern. My friend in psychology there has been of considerable help. The university has granted her a splendid scholarship, and she has been offered a position as student instructor and has accepted. Mary Ann cares about people. With her graduate degree in clinical psychology, treating disturbed children, she will be in a position to express her concern in a tangible and meaningful way.

You ask about John Buskin, whom Mary Ann has mentioned in her letters. He is a senior and headed for law school. A serious student, also on the quiet side. He and Mary Ann have been seeing each other regularly since last September. They have each other and apparently do not need a host of friends. As far as I know they are not engaged; they certainly do not intend to marry in the near future. But finding each other, at a critical period in their lives, has been their salvation. Mary Ann is reserved but—what many people do not realize—if given the chance, an extremely warm and responsive person. More than anyone I know, she needs the touch of a man and the security of being wanted by him. John is of somewhat the same temperament in being serious and retiring, but also friendly once you get to know him. All I can say is that they have been good for each other, and come June they will go their separate ways, Mary Ann to Northwestern and John to Harvard. You need not worry—there will be no repeat of the experience of two years ago. Now wiser in the ways of the world, Mary Ann says it should not have happened then and will never happen again, until she wants it to happen.

Mary Ann's faith is still clear and strong, and this is quite an achievement in the midst of the muddled condition of so many college students. She still believes in God, that God is love and love is of God; she believes in Jesus Christ, who by his life of suffering helps us understand the nature of God and man's achievement of meaning in life. She still believes in the church! Not as an institution or a place to go, but as people in the world who not only care but have discovered ways to express their love and concern for each other. As a child psychologist in a hospital or clinic, Mary Ann, with her understanding ways, her quiet manner, her magnificent intellect and perceptive spirit, will be doing the work of the church. She profoundly believes this.

Give me a ring as soon as you arrive, the number here is 624-8471. Though we have never met, I feel that I know you. It will be good to see you and your family in person.

Sincerely,

W. S.

VI

To Mrs. Sally Blanton,
concerning her daughter Sue

Rooms, Hours, and a Man's World

Dear Sally,

Your letter from Venice arrived while I was away from campus attending a special conference for college chaplains. I know you had an exciting trip. Tell Bud Morrison we miss him around here. He always took a personal interest in the students' ailments. Our new doctor in the clinic is a lost cause, I'm afraid. And he doesn't play tennis!

Sue appears well and happy. Her difficulty at the moment arises out of a dispute between her (along with several classmates) and the Dean of Women. Several months ago she was elected chairman of a special student committee to investigate and make recommendations concerning the use of women's dorm rooms by male students. Women students are permitted in men's rooms throughout the day and until ten o'clock on week nights and one on weekends. Men students are not permitted in girls' rooms at any hour, even during the day. Many women students consider this unreasonable and discriminatory.

Sue's committee held several meetings, lined up their proposals, and then went directly to the Dean of Women for a decision. The committee demanded equal rights for women, i.e., that male students should be allowed in women's rooms at precisely the same hours as vice versa. The Dean was adamant—men could not visit in women's rooms at any hour of the day or night. Following this decision the girls, led by Sue, organized a demonstration. At first, there was only mild picketing. Several girls carried signs which read, Equal rights for Kingston women! Sock it to 'em, Sue! and so forth.

Picketing led to a march with more than a thousand students, men and women, taking part. The demonstration lasted twenty-four consecutive hours, with classes suspended. Then came the climax. When the administration refused to meet with the students, several girls—juniors and seniors, led by Sue—marched into the Dean's waiting room and sat or lay down and blocked passage. The scheme was well planned. When one girl went to the bathroom, another took her place. Coffee and sandwiches were sneaked in to them, and the girls appeared to be having a ball. After two days of this take-over, police moved in and carried the girls out bodily. Sue and her committee were apprehended, driven to headquarters, and promptly released without any charges being filed against them.

The upshot of the matter is that the girls won a victory. The President, more liberal than the Dean of Women, agreed to sit in on subsequent discussions. The final decision was that men could be in women's rooms at precisely the same hours as girls in men's rooms. However, from the women's point of view there was one act of discrimination: when a woman entertains a man in her room, the door must be left open two inches. Since all girls have roommates, they have devised rules for certain dates. A white towel on the outside doorknob means, "I am entertaining, but you may enter—slowly." A red ribbon on the doorknob means, "Do not enter." The jokes about the celebrated two inches of door space are endless. Girls now carry short rulers with them as a reminder that there is still a difference between men and women and that this is a man's world.

As you know I live on campus, and I am able to make one observation. Since Sue and her committee won the battle of the rooms there is far less public exhibitionism between the sexes. Of course, there is still hand-holding or even arms around each other, but the open love-making, necking, and conjugal activity on the back lawn or behind the gym has virtually disappeared. (You remember when we were students, behind the gym was the favorite place.)

Your protest about the college permitting production of

Who's Afraid of Virginia Woolf is noted and carefully appraised. I am glad you didn't write Dean Blower; Sue has enough problems. Though in my judgment the play is overrated and overacclaimed, I still feel that it was a good thing for the dramatic department to attempt, and an excellent decision on the part of the college to permit it. If censorship invades the college campus, it can and will extend to all media. Where it will stop, no one knows. David and Bathsheba might be as objectionable to some people as *Virginia Woolf.*

You would have been proud of Sue, who had the second female lead. She was perfect for the part, but what astonished everyone was her almost professional power. Of course, she had had parts in several school productions, but this called for a genuine depth of acting ability. Sue was more than equal to it. She is a bright girl, and I only hope that direct communication between the two of you will be resumed in the very near future. Perhaps if you can come to Kingston this year or during her senior year, we can arrange a meeting in my office or at my house. After the long gap in your contact, I think Sue is really eager to get to know you again.

Yours,
W. S.

P.S. Sue burst into my office this morning livid with rage, and it was difficult for me to hide my amusement. You know, of course, that she is a fanatic on feminism and obsessed with the idea that society, including the church, discriminates against women. Last night she prepared a written assignment in medieval history and came across the famous statement of one of the popes concerning the church's opposition to coed colleges. It asserted that the church must be opposed to them because they "would lead to promiscuity" and—what was worse—to "equality of the sexes."

A Man Is a Good Thing To Have Around

DEAR SALLY,

Your forthcoming trip to Rio will, I am sure, be a stimulating adventure. If anything develops at this end of the line I will get in touch with you. It was thoughtful of you to send me your itinerary and addresses.

Sue does not give me the impression that she is boy-crazy. She likes men and certainly has no trouble in getting more dates than she can accept. If I were you, I would prefer this healthy condition to that of the "loner" or the girl who is limited to other girls for companionship. Though there are more men than women at Kingston, the dating problem has not changed since you were here. Kingston men import girls from surrounding colleges in great numbers. I do not know whether this is a status symbol or whether sex is easier and less complicated with "imports." However, Sue never lacks for dates, but this does not mean she is boy-crazy.

I cannot tell you about her relation to Larry Erickson. I have seen them together on campus a couple of times, but beyond that I simply do not know.

You say you are petrified since you heard that she and Larry are going steady. Though I can't comment on the dating, I can say something about Larry. He is no radical or criminal, as you suggest. He is the editor of the *Kingstonian*, a brilliant, committed, courageous and serious young man. He is antiwar and antidraft, and has tried to find ways of registering his protests. For picketing the chemical company which tried to recruit chemistry majors to work with luciform, etc., and for picketing the administration for accepting government grants for research in more sophisticated means of warfare, he was arrested, tried, convicted, and given a ninety-day suspended sentence. He feels that our tools of war in that torn little African country have already become demonic, and further, that it is not the business of a college or university to become a research center for the government in the area of methods and weapons of war. If the government must have such centers, let it establish them even as it has built military academies. Erickson is a young man trying to find ways of nonviolently protesting certain government policies and programs.

You insist that it would be better for him and all of the war-resisters to "support our fighting men." Sally, that is precisely what they are doing! They support our men, not by sending them more sophisticated weapons with which to kill and be killed, but by trying to bring them home. It has been three long years. We have lost more men than in Vietnam, we have spent more money than in Korea. Our being in the country at all seems to Larry a catastrophe of the first order. If this war had some meaning, some significant purpose, that would be one thing, but for many people (as well as government leaders) it has long ago lost any meaning or purpose.

You ask if I think Sue feels hostile toward you because of the divorce, or because Bud accompanied you to Rome and Venice. It is hard to say. From my own point of view, it would have been better if you had waited for your own divorce to become final. Sue has no hostility toward you, I think, because of the divorce itself. She tells me that ever since she was a little girl it has appeared inevitable. It is the story of two hopelessly incompatible people caught in the marriage web. He a professional man—head over heels in love with engineering; she a gay woman who wanted the world. Sue has no hostility toward you because of the divorce.

And believe it or not, she has no criticism of you or Bud because of the trips. Apparently you love the man, and Sue accepts this. However, her criticism of him is quite severe on another count, and I doubt that she will ever feel really cordial toward him. He was our best staff doctor here at Kingston. He always took a genuine interest in students and their mental and physical aches and pains. In other words, he had a practice and a ministry, but as of six months ago—since meeting you—he has announced his retirement from the practice of medicine at the age of forty-two, just when a doctor begins to know his craft! Sue cannot understand this or accept it. She says that with the critical shortage of doctors in this country, with poor and middle-income people being denied medical services, it is sacrilegious for a well-trained, healthy doctor to retire at that age. So at this point, though she seeks reconciliation with you, it will be another matter for Dr. Morrison.

Have a grand trip to Rio, and keep in touch.

Sincerely yours,

W. S.

P.S. Mrs. Morrison and the children left Kingston yesterday. They are moving to Phoenix. I know it is a relief to you that Bud's divorce is at last final.

Erecting Walls and Tearing Them Down

Dear Sally,

Welcome home! The trip to Rio must have been delightful. So your next cruise will be to Hong Kong on a "slow boat to China." I hope someday to have the opportunity of travel. There are many fascinating things to see in this world, new and strange cultures to study, and so many people to meet with backgrounds different from our own.

I regret very much that your divorce has been delayed. However, with so many investments and properties at stake, I can understand some of the complications. Tell Bud I miss him as a tennis partner more than ever. He was a good, hard player, and I must confess he "carried" me most of the time. I've found no one to take his place. The new doctor is past sixty and wants very much to retire. He has little interest in the students and often doesn't even show up for work. His practice makes a sad contrast with the high professional standards to which we became accustomed under Dr. Morrison.

You ask, "What is this nonsense about Sue resigning from Beta Beta Gamma?"

The local sorority—your own—pledged a Negro, contrary to national policy. The national governing body then suspended the local chapter. Sue and several of her sisters protested this. They took the case all the way to the national committee. But the committee would not budge—the sorority is Caucasian— no Negroes, no Jews. No federal law can touch this sacred principle in a private organization. Sue did not exactly resign; she and the local members voted to sever relations from the national. This was done last year. And this year, because of its purely local nature, Beta Beta Gamma has been unable to secure pledges. Who wants to join a sorority with no national standing?

Sue is living in the girls' dorm and appears to like it. I asked her about the sorority (which folded last month), and she said, "It's a good thing it died. If I had anything to do with it, I would close every sorority and every fraternity."

Having served two years as president, working hard to make Beta Beta Gamma the strongest on campus, I know this is a disappointment to you. I suppose you have met sisters all over the world.

However, the traditional concept of sororities and fraternities is being challenged by many of this generation of college students, who feel that the nation has enough units of exclusiveness without the college or university contributing to the greater proliferation. We have raised walls that separate us from each other—senseless walls. There are religious walls, political walls, social and financial walls. The question asked by some of today's college students is, "Why one more wall of exclusiveness?"

This is not to say that all students share this point of view. Some are as gung-ho about the fraternity-sorority system as our own generation was. They do the whole bit in securing pledges who meet their requirements in color and social standing; they take seriously the childish mumbo-jumbo of initiation; they still throw their big beer and liquor parties, and they still strive zealously to make "our sorority" or "our fraternity" the best on campus.

But the dynamic has gone out of the effort, and it has largely lost meaning to many young people like Sue. She is no longer a member of Beta Beta Gamma—she killed it here, and she couldn't care less.

Right now she is involved in a dispute with the faculty over the policy of ignoring student suggestions concerning the curriculum. Sue can get really steamed about this! The policy has never before been questioned at Kingston, and I shall be interested to see how far she gets with it. Certainly something should be done about the host of irrelevant, meaningless courses in the curriculum. The administration's hands are somewhat tied—especially as they deal with older professors who have tenure.

You will be interested to know that in my presence the other day, Sue made a comment about you. "My mother," she said, "is the greatest." By that she meant that in her judgment you are the most beautiful, the gayest, and the smartest woman in the world. You're "the greatest"—and she means it. Sue is ready and eager for some sort of reconciliation. When you return from Hong Kong, try to visit the campus for a few days. I realize it will be a little awkward for Bud to come with you, but by that time your divorce may be final and you can come as Mrs. Morrison. In the meantime, I will try to help Sue accept him, though it may not be easy.

Sincerely yours,

W. S.

P.S. Sue's efforts with the curriculum committee have created a considerable amount of cross-fire between the administration and the faculty. The administration is pleased that students are pressing for a voice in determining the direction of the curriculum but it looks with disfavor upon students who attempt to determine administrative policy. The faculty, on the other hand, strongly favors student participation in the administration of policy while, at the same time, it is horrified at the thought that students would have even the slightest responsibility for determining courses of study. All of this means that people are wide open to change except when their own little world is threatened!

Laws Will Change but Customs Never— Well, Almost Never

DEAR SALLY,

Yes, this is Sue's final year and I know how relieved you will be. She has been the cause of many an anxious moment for you, but in the main her record has been outstanding.

I cannot fully answer your question about Sue's refusal to accept the nomination as this year's Homecoming Queen. As you know, she was one of the "five loveliest" nominated. In my judgment she might have easily been picked as queen. She is bright and vivacious and also a recognized campus leader. I asked her about the contest and she simply said, "It's for the birds." She felt it was in the same class as all the Miss America beauty contests held around the country. She would not display her flesh (she said rather haughtily) as if she were in a dog show, nor would she consider it an honor to be selected. You say that when you were here you would have been overwhelmed at being nominated and would have given anything—anything— to be named. I can't fully answer the question, "What has got into our children?" But I do know that many of them simply have a different set of values from those we had.

There is a freedom about Sue that most of us secretly envy. This fall she put her Jaguar in the garage and bought a full-sized motorcycle. I must admit the roar of the thing, not to mention the speed, frightens me. But your friends need not alarm you; she is perfectly capable of handling the machine and taking care of herself. Only yesterday I saw her flying down Locust Street with Larry Erickson doubling behind. Their wave to me was a reminder that they had the situation under control.

Not many years ago a "nice" girl did not ride on a motorcycle, much less buy one and drive it herself. Times have changed. There is a new burst of freedom in the land. This thirst for freedom sometimes applies to laws; "Freedom Now" is the chant and the motto. But the freedom Sue and Larry are determined to achieve is *freedom from customs*. For customs can be more binding than laws. In their personal lives young people are demanding to be freed from customs which may have meant something to us but mean little to them.

Customs relating to dress, music, dance, art, drama, language, hair, love, sex and marriage, and so on are being challenged. And I predict that in the future many more of them will change.

I asked a student the other day to explain to me the fanatical response to rock-and-roll music. His answer was revealing. "I'm not sure we like it all that well—but it's ours: the people who write it, the people who play it, the people who sing it—are ours. We created this music, we love it because it belongs to us—and also because 'old' people don't like it."

Concerning the delicate matter that really prompted your last letter and which has caused you such embarrassment with your Kingston friends, I have little to offer by way of explanation. Your classmate, Jane Grabling, is quite correct—no doubt as a professor's wife she sees a good deal of what goes on. It is true that Sue and Larry have "shacked up." They have taken an apartment. It is policy to permit seniors to live off campus. They are now nearly twenty-two years of age. It should not be surprising to us that Sue would do such a thing. You started her in dancing school at four; she had, with your permission, regular dates at eleven. She is precocious, well developed, and emotionally more mature than almost any girl on campus.

She will not get pregnant, I feel very sure. Sue went to one of the town's best gynecologists—not on the college staff—and told him she was getting married. In her view, she and Larry are married—not in the conventional sense, but married none the less. The doctor gave her a thorough physical examination and prescribed the pills. The administration knows about Sue and Larry as it knows about several other senior couples. But the policy here is to do nothing and say nothing unless someone objects. I have counseled Larry's parents—poor, hard-working, churchgoing people—to remain quiet, and I suggest you do the same. You cannot change the basic facts. Sue and Larry have just a little more than one semester left before graduation—it would be a pity to spoil it.

It's too bad that your trip to India has been delayed. I hope for your sake that Blanton does not cause any more trouble than necessary about the divorce. Of course, as you say, he can make difficulties; the situation with Bud has not always been handled as discreetly as possible.

Tell Mrs. Grabling to cool it, that you have accepted things as they are and for her to keep as quiet as possible.

Sincerely yours,

W. S.

The Long Arm of the Past

DEAR SALLY,

Your recent note raised the question of whether or not I hold any hidden feelings of hostility toward you. As far as I know I don't, and the reason is simple. Things have a way of working out for the best. During our college years, you and I were sure we were in love and for all practical purposes we were engaged. You—not I—broke the engagement, and you broke it for only one reason: Sally Horton could not marry a man who intended to become a minister. In some ways you could imagine me as a minister, but in a thousand years you could not see yourself as a minister's wife. And so it ended and we went our separate paths.

In marrying Blanton, you did well in a variety of ways. In the ministry I have had my ups and downs. Many times I have wondered whether I chose well. It is no bed of roses. The preacher image is difficult to live with, and the petty problems I often deal with are irritating to a person who would rather be creative. The limited salary has imposed harsh limitations on one who would relish seeing and enjoying the world. But from an over-all perspective—the long view—I'm glad I chose as I did. The rewards are quiet and subtle, but I assure you they are most satisfying.

You ask (as you have before) if Sue knows about us—our attachment and engagement. Of course she knows the vague circumstances, but not the actual story—certainly not its outcome. She knows that while you were at Kingston and I at State we dated, but she definitely does not know that we were ever engaged. Once she laughed and said, "What a joke it would have been if my mother had married a preacher!"

Speaking of Sue, it is difficult for me not to show partiality. With her I sometimes find myself in the role not of chaplain but of parent. She causes me considerable distress because among other things she refuses to study. She is a B student, but with a little effort she could lead her class. However, she prefers to work for causes and to become involved with the world. She has forced the student body to question the existence of sororities and fraternities. She has forced the administration and student body to reevaluate and examine all the hoopla in connection with the election of various sorts of "queens." She led the fight for the right of women to use their rooms the same hours and in the same manner as do men. She killed compulsory chapel singlehanded; it was her stubbornness, her determination, that finally brought the issue before the full faculty. Of course, the faculty gleefully voted to discontinue compulsory chapel, but this was only the beginning. It had to be approved by the Board of Trustees. On behalf of the student body, Sue appeared before that august tribunal and made her point: "No state and no institution can compel anyone to worship God."

For many reasons I know these have been anxious days for you. Surely Blanton should see the handwriting on the wall and give you the divorce. I don't see what he can gain by contesting it; it will only mean embarrassment to both of you. Try to look on the brighter side. He may yet be generous and withdraw his objections. Whatever happens, I hope he will show a little interest in Sue. She needs a father. And by that I mean she needs more than a bank account.

Sincerely,
W. S.

The Winter of Hope and the Spring of Despair

DEAR MRS. MORRISON!

Congratulations!

I know you and the doctor will be happy. You have so much in common and so much to live for. I am ecstatic about Bud's decision to return to the college and the clinic. Not only shall I once more have an excellent tennis partner, but the college will regain the services of the best general practitioner in the business. I hope you overstated the situation when you said that after two years he is fed up with running around the world; but I can't tell you how delighted I am that he wants his job back.

Sue was in the office today and she is excited. Of course she knows Doc Morrison, but until he decided to go back to work I am sure she would never really have accepted him. But now she is looking forward to seeing and meeting her "new father." You should be happy with the developments.

Sue has just won another battle with the administration. Junior and senior students will be invited to sit on various curriculum committees, not to force certain subjects down the throats of the faculty, but to make suggestions concerning students' needs, interests, and desires. As you know, professors in various departments do get into deep ruts. Some of them have been reading the same lectures to successive generations of students for twenty years. With seniority and tenure, no one, not even the President, can touch them. But I think they will be responsive to student thinking and demands.

Larry Erickson's situation could get serious this week. As you know, he was arrested, tried, and convicted last year on two counts. He and a number of other students objected to the chemical company's recruitment of students and also to the college's acceptance of a government grant for research in the field of more sophisticated warfare. He was sentenced to ninety days, but the judge suspended it. Next Sunday, Larry and his associates on the staff of the *Kingstonian* are planning a "burn-in." They will publicly burn their draft cards, which is of course now considered a criminal offense. If they go through with it, he could get a stiff penalty. His conviction last year would predetermine that.

It is only two months to commencement, and I hope that Larry and Sue will be permitted to graduate no matter what happens. I talked to Sue about the "burn-in" next Sunday and she says it was her idea! That is, for the seniors to find some way to protest—dramatically, nonviolently, ultimately. The love that exists between these two young people is an inspiration to me. Sue laughed and quoted from *A Tale of Two Cities*, "It was the best of times, it was the worst of times . . . it was the spring of hope and the winter of despair." Then she said, "The *winter* of hope and the *spring* of despair." If Larry goes to the penitentiary, she will wait for him—and she means it.

Give me a ring when you get here next week. Helen and I will be delighted to see you both.

Sincerely yours,
W. S.

VII
To Mr. and Mrs. Erickson, concerning their son Larry

Bad Words and Long Hair

DEAR MR. AND MRS. ERICKSON,

As you requested, I went to see Dean Blower about your son's recent suspension. It appears that the situation is not as serious as you first thought, and I am sure Larry will be writing to you within the next few weeks.

During Larry's more than two years at Kingston he has made an excellent record. He is a better-than-average student, is liked by his classmates, respected by most of the faculty, and as editor of the *Kingstonian* has done a superb job.

In the last issue of the paper he ran an editorial (which he wrote himself) in defense of the drama department's production of *Who's Afraid of Virginia Woolf*. In it he used a number of words which the Dean felt were obscene. Our weekly paper goes to various colleges over the country, but it is also read by a large number of alumni and of course by members of the Board of Trustees. Dean Blower felt that this particular issue would offend many people connected with the college. Thus the paper was confiscated, distribution withheld, and the editor suspended.

During our conversation the Dean revealed that he has no intention of punishing Larry severely. He simply wants to let the alumni and trustees know that "so long as I am Dean this sort of thing will not be tolerated at Kingston." He has assured Larry that his suspension is a matter of merely a few days. However, he is trying to exact a promise that this type of editorial (using "obscene" words) will not be repeated.

At this point we may have a little trouble. As you know, Larry is a lad who, when he makes up his mind, is hard to sway. I doubt that he will make any such promise. Thus the situation could get sticky, but I predict that your son will come out on top.

I talked with Larry about the editorial, and the explanation was that in his opinion the drama department did an excellent job in presenting the difficult play Who's Afraid of Virginia Woolf. The play dealt with college people—real people with real problems who used strong language. But Larry insists that it is language almost universally used by people in various walks of life. He laughed and said that he had heard his father, on more than one occasion, use the identical language printed in the editorial. Now the interesting point is: If, indeed, such language is known and used by college professors, housewives, and salesmen, it would be strange if it could not be found occasionally in a play or movie.

Why do certain words repel us, while others in fact much more repulsive do not? Many people are not outraged by "nigger," "kike," or "dago." By some these terms are even regarded as amusing. I suppose your generation and mine is "hung up" on anything pertaining to the basic act of sex, while we take naturally any vulgarity involving our dealing with people unlike ourselves.

Larry is a straightforward boy. In writing the editorial he was simply being honest and direct. I sometimes feel that many of us have become so accustomed to evasion that we are more offended by honesty than we are by the words and symbols used. At any rate you need have no excessive worries about Larry at this time. His suspension will be lifted before the week's out and he will go back to the routine of classwork as well as getting out the next issues of the Kingstonian. My suggestion is that you ignore the incident as much as possible. If the Dean notifies you, answer him politely and with concern. If Larry mentions the suspension, then of course you will reply, and perhaps let him know that you do not consider the matter of earth-shaking proportions. If he does not mention it, by all means let the matter drop.

You ask me something else about which I can give little information. Sue Blanton is a junior, a pixy of a girl with a fiery determination to correct what she considers abuses on campus. She has a great flair for life and is extremely popular with the boys, dating a different one each week. Larry's pattern has been more or less similar. He, too, has played the field. After all, he is a very attractive young man. You say that one of his former girl friends has brought you up to date on the latest developments at Kingston, including the rumor that Larry and Sue (whom you describe as wild and irresponsible) have settled down to going steady, and that they are serious. I have not talked to either one of them about this, and if I had I would be reluctant to discuss it without their permission. After all, both Larry and Sue are approaching twenty-one—they are not children in junior high.

In closing I must comment on one other point in your letter. Long hair on boys has become an emotional hang-up for most parents. You say you are not opposed to it, but only to what it stands for. From your point of view it means that a boy is effeminate or a hippie. Knowing Larry's interest in the girls should put your mind at ease concerning the first point. The second is even more out of character. Your son is no hippie. Hippies represent only a small segment of the youth of this country. They have become so disillusioned with the life we adults have created that they have rejected it—have literally dropped out. Larry and the young people who share his point of view want just the opposite; they don't want to drop out but to participate. They do not expect to control or run the country, but they do want a voice in its operation. There is much in the life of our nation to which they object, but rejecting life and running away is the last thing they will do. Larry is no hippie, and even if he lets his hair grow down to his shoulders (which so far he has not done) he will never be one.

Parents' Weekend comes the latter part of next month. If you can visit the campus at that time, I hope you will drop by the office and say hello. If I can be of further help, kindly let me know.

Sincerely yours,
W. S.

Faith Is a Piece of the Action

Dear Mr. and Mrs. Erickson,

Your recent letter expressing gratitude for what I did for Larry is deeply appreciated.

It was very little, really, yet my character testimony seems to have had some influence on the judge. A number of people thought Larry's ninety-day sentence was a bit severe; then, when the judge suspended it, we were all relieved. I am sorry illness prevented you from attending the trial, but I know that though you may not always agree with what your son says and does you are with him in spirit. He is your son, you love him, and he loves you. Never let anything take that from you.

I believe what I said on the witness stand about Larry. He is a young man with compassion and courage, character and integrity, and he has demonstrated these qualities in more ways than one. When the prosecuting attorney asked if I agreed with Larry's editorial comments on Virginia Woolf, I could only say that this was his way of being honest and straightforward. I'm not sure I see the relation of Virginia Woolf to the incidents that brought Larry to trial, but I suppose the attorney was trying to make the point that a person who would use such language would resort to anything, including devious ways to oppose the war!

Larry's experience with the law, his arrest, and his willingness to go to jail for his beliefs have had two basic effects on me. First, I see as never before the striking difference between the talkers and the doers. Talkers and counselors like myself seldom create consternation among the natives, for the simple reason that they do not believe us until we act. Writing, I suppose, is a form of action, but it is quite clear that a writer—even a committed writer—can hide behind his typewriter and seal himself off from the community. True, the pen is in certain instances mightier than the sword. But this is an overplayed cliché—suppose you live in a country where people never read (we may be fast becoming such a country)? Men in the pulpit as well as editors may denounce or praise certain laws or programs. They may endorse or recommend specific action, but the time will come when no one will pay any attention to what they say unless they are willing to act.

Many missionaries years ago lost their influence over many of the people they served because they refused to identify with them in their need. The only effective poverty worker is the man or woman who is willing to live with those in poverty. There are various reasons for the colossal failure of the government's poverty program. Among them, I may note that it is difficult for a man to earn an exorbitant income, live in luxury, and identify with those who suffer from malnitrition, dilapidated housing, and a lack of medical services. The same is true of the man who is for peace and against military involvement.

As editor of the college paper, Larry holds what is perhaps the most influential student position on campus. He could have sat back, writing his blazing editorials and perhaps stirring up a little flack from the administration, trustees, and alumni. But when he *acted*, he really struck fire. Concerned people, both pro and con, took him seriously.

In the *Kingstonian* he expressed the paper's opposition to recruitment of chemistry majors to work in perfecting luciform and other demonic means of warfare. He said he saw little difference between incinerating people in the bunkers and villages of a small African country and the Nazi annihilation of Jews in concentration camps. He further opposed the government grant to the college for research into more sophisticated and devastating means of warfare. After writing these rather strong statements he acted, and he tried to act—to protest—in a nonviolent manner. He picketed and led demonstrations and marches, and these in turn led to the fury and violence of certain townspeople who support the current war effort. The result was that Larry was beaten by the opposing mob and arrested for instigating a riot. His trial was held this morning, and, as I told you, he received a suspended sentence.

The second effect of Larry's actions is to force me to re-evaluate my own position and faith. Faith, it seems to me as never before, is not the acceptance or endorsement of a creed or a person; faith is to act. *Action is not the result of faith, it is faith*. In other words, what I am saying is, my own conscience has been touched by the life of your son. He is making me think, he is making me uncomfortable, and I believe he is making me a better person.

No, he did not have his hair cut for the trial, and I am sure this was a point against him. The townspeople (who share your point of view about long hair) would have convicted and jailed him on the spot. But I don't think Larry is about to have his hair cut (crew or otherwise). Very short hair—"war hair"— did not become a standard for men until after World War I. It increased in popularity after World War II. Larry feels that his hair is a silent but visible protest against what is wrong in our society.

With best of wishes, I am

Sincerely yours,
W. S.

"Their" Morals and "Our" Morals

DEAR MR. AND MRS. ERICKSON,

It is too bad that you could not attend Parents' Weekend. Most of the excitement concerning Larry's arrest and trial has subsided around here. You say that in your own community during the past several weeks it has created even more pressure. I know your embarrassment is real, as you meet with your fellow church members, friends, and neighbors. But it will do little good to mention this to Larry. Let him know that you love him, even though you may disagree with what he is doing.

Larry's convictions are based on what he considers moral grounds. I have already outlined them to you in my last letter and doubt whether I can make them any clearer.

It is interesting to me, a minister, to hear a young man with no apparent faith in God strive so zealously for the moral life. You are devout Methodists, whereas Larry claims no church affiliation. Two years ago, when he was a freshman, he wrote an article for the *Kingstonian* concerning our nation's involvement in the present war. At that time there were stirrings and grumblings among people who were getting restless about our war efforts, but no general uprising. Larry's article viewed our African intervention as a repetition of the war in Vietnam—as not only a tactical blunder but also an *immoral* act. It is wrong, he thinks, for us to inject military power into a situation of civil war; it is wrong for us to defend a corrupt government which has little or no support from its own people; it is wrong for us to enlarge the conflict by using every form of highly developed weapon—including personnel bombs and luciform—against a backward, agrarian people.

Well, of course, the tide is turning. Many leaders are now opposed to our involvement in Africa. But the reasons are quite different from Larry's. Politicians (with the exception of the President) no longer speak with enthusiasm about our "defense of freedom." Military men now say our strategy was bad and we cannot win a military victory. But the topper has been the change of attitude among businessmen. In three years we have poured 120 billion dollars into that small country. This has overheated our economy, causing false prosperity, serious inflation, and the economic destruction of our own older people who must live on fixed incomes. Our diplomats now lament the loss of allies and—what is more desolating—the support of those small underground groups in all the iron-curtain countries who a few years ago looked to the United States as a "nation of hope" and now see us as barbarians. It was Larry who recently pointed out that even in Russia men like the poet Yetushenko and the writer Vosnesensky have joined world-wide criticism of our efforts. Once men like these took their lives in their hands in order to criticize their own Communist governments, and supported us as the "hope of freedom." Now these few friendly voices in iron-curtain countries have taken on stinging tones of rebuke.

I'm elaborating on all this to help you understand that your son is a moral person who is committed to moral issues. Morality to him is not strategy, economics, or a pragmatic relation with our allies. Morality concerns the "rightness" or "wrongness" of specific actions. I am sure people of your generation—and mine

—hold certain moral commitments about which we can become excited or indignant. We must therefore try to understand Larry's position. We must remember that, though his set of values may be different from ours, he feels just as strongly about them.

You can see now why I have kept on insisting that your son is no hippie. The latter have "copped out." Hippies sneer at society's blunders; they want no part of us, yet they seek to correct no evils, heal no wounds, nor do they work for justice. They laugh, live, and copulate in the midst of filth and the fog of various narcotics. But, Mr. and Mrs. Erickson, *that* is not your son. He believes that though this nation has made a great blunder in Africa, it is basically both strong and good; it can yet make its finest humanitarian contribution.

So Larry's beliefs are rooted in morality, and these are the toughest kind. He wants your support, but whether you are with or against him, he will not be deterred.

Sincerely,
W. S.

A Wee Bit of Encouragement from the Church

DEAR MR. AND MRS. ERICKSON,

Just a note to say that I am delighted to hear that you are feeling better about Larry and his activities at Kingston. Your friends at church have apparently hurt and embarrassed you. However, it is good to know that you have resumed going to Sunday service and are able to handle the coolness of friends and fellow members.

It was thoughtful of your pastor to come to see you. Even

though he was guarded in what he said, you apparently received the impression that he was on Larry's side. It is a pity that he has proclaimed nothing from the pulpit to indicate this, but I know you are grateful for his personal encouragement.

Your pastor, of course, is not alone. The pulpit in this country has either been silent about our massacre in Africa, or has talked out of both sides of its mouth. Only in rare instances do we see pastor and people preach and act in a prophetic manner. At any rate, I am glad your pastor has some reservations about our current military involvement.

Larry came by the office this morning and said he would write you sometime this week. He has just landed a job for the summer working for one of the "peace" senators in Washington. This means that you will not see much of him, but he will be doing what means most to him.

Sincerely,
W. S.

"Shacking Up"

DEAR MR. AND MRS. ERICKSON,

Things appeared to be going more smoothly between you and Larry, and now here they are, worse than ever! I understand that you have threatened to discontinue his tuition as well as his allowance.

Larry told me the other day that he would rather not write you about the latest development in his personal life, but certainly had no objection to my doing so. Thus I have his permission to reply to your urgent letter and give you my impressions.

Your informant appears to be correct as to the facts she passed along to you. Larry and Sue Blanton are not simply going together but are living together. In September, when they returned to Kingston, they found a modest apartment within walking distance of the college. Sue has an almost unlimited income. Believe me, she is very far from being a promiscuous slut. She is a bright, sensitive, and lovable girl, and like Larry a strong campus leader. Both she and Larry turned twenty-one this summer. They are old enough to know at least in some degree what they are doing, and they are willing to take criticism, and possible expulsion, as a result of their actions.

You ask about the policy of the college in such cases. During the past several years a number of seniors have chosen to do what Larry and Sue have done. The official policy is, of course, opposed to such behavior. However, unless someone raises an objection, it goes unquestioned. The college has enough problems with hippies, beatniks, demonstrations, riots, and so forth without attempting to straighten out or suppress the love life of two people as stable as Larry and Sue. I suggest that you refrain from calling this to the attention of the administration. It knows precisely what is happening in their case. If you in any way contact Dean Blower or anyone else about the matter, they will be forced to act, and in such instances the action is rather harsh. Otherwise Larry and Sue will get through the year, graduate, and go on their way.

Again, you raise the question of morality. The practice here illustrates the great chasm that exists between some members of this generation and their parents. Morality to Larry, as I have said before, is a serious subject. He thinks of it in terms of such matters as killing (as we are doing in Africa); as economic exploitation (of migrants, sharecroppers, and in certain instances schoolteachers); as racial oppression (not simply in Mississippi and Alabama, but in Chicago, Los Angeles, and Newark).

These are moral issues and Larry feels deeply about them. However, Larry feels that love and sex do not become moral questions unless or until abuse and exploitation are involved. He feels that between consenting adults, love and sex are personal questions and should not be regulated either by law or custom.

I suppose we have two approaches to morality going here. One is a concern for justice and the other involves breaking a rule, code, or commandment. Your son is concerned about the first; he could not care less about the second.

Writing in the *Kingstonian*, he recently explained his position on this matter. The editorial was entitled "Law, Custom, and Marriage." He said that certain laws are necessary, but they must be justified by three criteria. First, good laws are made by representatives of the people and not by a dictator—not even a "benevolent" dictator. Second, laws must serve a definite purpose, i.e., must accomplish the greatest good for the most people, while at the same time protecting the rights of minority groups. In other words, laws must exist for the welfare of people. Third, when laws no longer serve their purpose, they must be changed or withdrawn. Larry feels (and has said so many times in the *Kingstonian*) that many of the laws on our books which seek to control love, marriage, and sex do not serve the best interests of the people. Birth control information and methods are an illustration. After many arduous years of struggle, protests, fighting, jail, and even bloodshed, most birth-control laws have finally been stricken from the books in this country. Contraceptives are freely available, and are used by virtually our entire adult population, including Roman Catholics.

Larry insists that most laws which seek to control love, marriage, and sex are as outmoded as laws on birth control. The older generation has simply not seen it yet—but in time they will. Your son believes that two people are not married by applying to the state for a license (as for hunting or fishing);

they are not married by a minister's pronouncement of a prayer over them. Shotgun marriages and marriages of financial convenience attest to this. Marriage, according to Larry, takes place only when two people give themselves to each other in love. This is the sacrament that binds them together. He feels that neither the state nor the church can add one ounce of meaning to such a relationship. He concluded the article by saying that the commitment of love between a man and a woman could be accompanied by a simple vow, a mutual covenant, and a significant symbol such as beads, a ring, or a peace medallion.

After this particular editorial appeared, and after I learned of the "relationship," I called Larry and we went over to the Sweet Shoppe for a coke. I told him I was concerned about the "arrangement" and asked him a simple question: Will he and Sue ever get married in the conventional sense—license, minister, and so on? He laughed and said he did not think so. His future, with his militant opposition to the war, is quite precarious, and he does not see that a license would help the situation. Furthermore, both he and Sue want to find some way of dramatizing their protest against what they consider an antiquated approach to love, sex, and marriage. My guess is that within a few years they will change their minds, but this is the way they feel now.

I know how difficult it is for you to accept what Larry and Sue are doing. It seems a threat to the American home, the foundation of our society, and it is a greater threat to every woman who wants the security of marriage by law. Yet, our divorce rate being what it is, and our extra-marital sex practices among both young people and adults being what they are, it is open to doubt as to whether Larry and Sue's approach is really the greater threat. If we cannot accept the life they have chosen, we must at least find it in our hearts to accept them. They are wonderful young people, and it would be a pity at this stage of their lives to cut them off from us.

There are many college students, as well as other young people in our country, who will not follow your children's way. But the sex code of your generation and mine seems to be becoming a thing of the past. It is now being disregarded by many as if it had never existed. If today's young people do not violate the code by "shacking up," many of them violate it in other ways—in many instances ways more destructive than that chosen by Larry and Sue.

Think it over and talk to your minister. He sounds like a reasonable sort of person.

Sincerely,
W. S.

A Protest—Open, Nonviolent, Ultimate

DEAR MR. AND MRS. ERICKSON,

Your call last night prompts this immediate letter. Simply by indicating that you will stand by Larry, you have come through in a grand way. It is a day of reconciliation.

Now to answer your question as to what took place yesterday morning in our chapel. What happened at Kingston is happening all over the United States, especially on college campuses. In chronological order, here is the sequence of events.

Larry and three of his associates on the staff of the *Kingstonian* came by my office last Monday and announced that they had decided to protest the war and the draft, openly and nonviolently. All four are seniors and will be eligible for the draft in two months. They wanted to know which I thought would be the most effective way of registering their protest: to collect as many draft cards as possible and return them to Washington with a letter saying, "Hell, no, we won't go!" or to hold a public service in the chapel, where those who await the draft would come forward and burn their cards. I asked each of the four boys if he had made up his mind that some form of open, non-violent protest must be made and each answered, "Yes." I suggested that a service be held in the chapel, at which time an invitation would be given to those facing the draft to come forward and burn their cards.

Announcements throughout the week had been made on campus and in town. The chapel was filled, several protest songs were sung, and a sense of spiritual or religious urgency gripped the congregation. The invitation was given and a number of young men came forward. Ashes from the cards were reverently deposited in a chalice used at the communion service. Somehow, I thought this was particularly appropriate.

Two FBI men and several local detectives were present. Larry and his three associates were immediately arrested and the names of the other students registered. The four boys were taken to jail, where they remained overnight; bail was arranged this morning and lawyers secured. The case will be called in the latter part of May. Thus the men will miss graduation exercises, but they are prepared to go to the penitentiary rather than participate in this brutal and meaningless war.

The entire college, including the administration, Dean Blower, faculty, and students, has risen to the support of Larry and his friends. It is reported that Kingston will lose millions of dollars because of the militant antiwar effort on campus. However, as Dean Blower said, "There are some things in life worth more than money."

I am glad you will be here for the trial. Be prepared for the worst. Larry will be harshly dealt with because of his conviction last year. I can only say that the people of this nation will one day look back in horror upon the atrocities we have committed, not merely in Africa, but here at home upon many of the finest young men in the country who resisted the war effort. Perhaps one day it will be said of them, "You saved us when we could not save ourselves."

As for myself, the rumors are flying that I shall be arrested and charged with counseling young men to evade the draft. The knock on the door may come any day or night. If so, I shall reluctantly leave my wife and children, but because of lessons learned during the past several years, I am prepared for whatever may come.

Sincerely yours,
W. S.

VIII

To Dean Blower,
concerning his son Bobby
and sundry matters

You're a Good Man, Dean Blower, But—

DEAR DEAN BLOWER,

I suppose this is a letter of resignation. This is not what I want but I can see no other way out. I have enjoyed ten exciting years here at Kingston and I would not exchange jobs with anyone.

Everything you say about Chaplain Croy, except your primary charge against him, is true. He has adopted many hippie customs, but he is no hippie. I will try to explain to you as I have to a number of parents: a beard does not a hippie make, nor does a mini-mini dress, nor language, nor certain rejections of "our" code of conduct. A hippie is a person who looks at the society we adults have created and then vomits. He rejects it, he hates it, he wants no part of it. He does not want our type of education, our family life, including the way we copulate, our work, our recreation, our houses, our gadgets, our swimming pools, our country clubs, our religion, and especially he does not want our politics, which he sees as monstrous hypocrisies. He is not simply disenchanted; he has disengaged himself from the society which spawned him.

There are thousands of high-school and college-age young people who adopt certain hippie customs and values, especially as to dress, hair, music, art, etc. However, these young people have not disengaged themselves and do not want to drop out; they want a piece of the action, they want to participate. The recent involvement of hundreds of college young people in the peace movement which has swept this country is an illustration. A few years ago we were complaining about the indifference and apathy of college students. Today many of them are involved in local and national politics. They are concerned about discrimination and injustice and they are trying to do something about the grinding poverty that touches forty million people in this affluent society.

This is what I have been trying to tell the administration here at Kingston for ten years. We are not dealing with junior high-school students who must be watched and supervised every hour of the day, and we are not dealing with the apathetic student generation of a few years ago. We are dealing with something that is alive with excitement and hope; we are dealing with young people who have both intelligence and integrity. They want a voice in what goes on in this country—and at Kingston. Why should they not sit on curriculum planning committees? Why should not the faculty-student congress be more than a mouthpiece for the administration? Why should they tolerate compulsory chapel? (Can anyone be compelled to worship God?) Why should they not be heard concerning the use of their rooms?

In recent years a number of our students have openly protested the erection of two new buildings: the football stadium and the chapel. As you well know, in both instances my sympathies were with the students. I felt their judgment was wiser than that of the alumni and the administration. With the decline of interest in football, the old stadium was more than adequate; with the decline of attendance at worship services, the old chapel was more than sufficient for our needs. The alumni (and the administration went along with them) naïvely felt that a new chapel with a new organ would increase student attendance!

So Chaplain Croy looks like a hippie and in certain ways acts like one, but *he and his followers are not hippies.* They want "in," they want to work, to give, to share, to participate. My good old friend, what else could we expect? Ever since Sputnik went up we have frantically accelerated our courses in all the lower grades and have made stronger demands on young people. Should it really surprise us, having given them the "grown-up" treatment for twelve years, that in college they want to be accepted as grown up, or as at least semiadult?

I understand that Mrs. Melvin Van Brock, Sr. has indicated that she will give no more money to the college until Chaplain Croy is fired. I suspect this information had more to do with your asking for his resignation than even his hippie ways. Your letter to him should also have been sent to me. If he goes, I go. My term of contract will end simultaneously with his. If you desire a personal conference about this I will be glad to talk to you. However, I assure you my mind is made up. There can be no deals, no accommodations. If Chaplain Croy is forcibly removed from his position, my contract at Kingston is automatically terminated.

Sincerely,
W. S.

No Indispensable Man

Dear Dean Blower,

You indicate that the college can get along without Chaplain Croy and without me. I have never presumed to think otherwise. There are dozens of qualified clergy waiting and eager to take our places. Kingston, with its academic standing, salary scale, and exciting student body, is a challenge to any minister. You are correct in stating that, though I have tenure, I have no case to present to the AAUP, since I was not fired but resigned. Of course Chaplain Croy, being an assistant chaplain and instructor in religion, has no recourse.

In my judgment, you are unfairly dismissing a young minister and are being unduly influenced by the practical threats of a neurotic woman. It seems to me that Kingston should be bigger than this. The college is strong enough to absorb the unconventional ways of a young minister, and it can get along without nervous right-wing money. During these past years Kingston has grown from obscurity until it is now one of the strongest schools in the East. The future is bright.

I can only say, also, that I regret very much the loss of a relationship which I cherished.

Sincerely,
W. S.

Reinstatement on Uneasy Terms

DEAR DEAN BLOWER,

I was as surprised as you when both faculty and student body rose to the defense of Chaplain Croy and myself. I am sorry that they felt it necessary to use the threat of prolonged demonstrations and strikes to win their point. I suppose you are right: with all the unrest on college campuses today, it would be foolish for Kingston to risk disruption over such an innocent matter as firing or retaining two lowly chaplains.

Of course, since Chaplain Croy has been reinstated I will reconsider my resignation, and shall do so in a hurry. You know as well as I that I did not want to leave. However, more than "being back on the job" I would like to feel that I have your good will and support. By contrast with most college campuses, the faculty here appears unanimous in its backing what we, in the chapel and the Department of Religion, are trying to do. I earnestly desire this same support from you and the other members of the administration.

There are times when I give the impression that I am "with" the students more than I am "with" the administration. I assure you that often just the opposite is true. Last year I openly opposed students who attempted to burn the ROTC headquarters. This was a serious act of violence. I also opposed certain student groups which sought to make fraternities and sororities sanctuaries for smoking marijuana. However, I shall continue to press for a greater voice of students in administrative affairs. I support the plan of permitting senior students to grade professors as well as members of the administration (including the chaplains). I shall continue to act as if I believed academic freedom were more important than buildings, and student freedom more important than a "respectable" reputation.

I'm glad I'm back.

Sincerely,
W. S.

Oh, To Be Wanted!

Dear Dean Blower,

It is most unfortunate that my friend at Ambler let the cat out of the bag. Yes, I was offered the job there, but for various reasons preferred to keep the offer secret. If it will relieve your apprehension, I turned it down. I am happy here. I have the support of the faculty and students and to some degree the administration. What more could I ask?

I can see your point. It's true that the campus is still somewhat tense, and no doubt the students would interpret my leaving as pressure from the administration. There are still elements of difference between us, on the war as well as a number of campus issues, and it may be true that the students are only too ready to demonstrate and perhaps riot at the drop of a hat (or a clerical robe).

Once again, let me say that I regret this type of blackmail has been used on you. Some day I want you to be able to say that you want me at Kingston because you want me.

At any rate I'm not accepting any new job. I'm staying.

Sincerely,

W. S.

The End of Blackmail

DEAR DEAN BLOWER,

I'm a happy man!

How I admire your public reversal of position on the war and your willingness to go to bat for Larry Erickson and me. That took courage! *Moral* courage— In the face of criticism from the alumni, the Board of Trustees, members of the administration, and wealthy contributors, it was a glorious act! I feel like a rejected suitor who has heard the girl of his dreams say, "Yes." And all cheerfulness aside, I don't underestimate the strength needed to risk ridicule and censure for changing your position.

I had a letter from Chaplain Croy the other day. He is pleased with his important job at Wellsfleet and says to give you his regards. He feels that "old Blower" has the capacity for bridging the generation gap.

During spring vacation, let's plan a day in New York with our wives—dinner and theater?

Sincerely,

W. S.

Another Generation Is Yet To Come

DEAR TOM,

Your note of appreciation for what I tried to do for Bobby is more than I deserve. It was no more than you would have done for my son under similar circumstances. Young Bob simply got in with a "hip" crowd, and before he knew it he was in over his head. The East Village is certainly no place for a eighteen-year-old who has known the shelter of a good home.

Of course you will do what you think best. There are twelve days of the conference left. You can leave London now or stick it out and make your appearance on the program. I hope you do the latter. I had a long talk with Bobby, and he is genuinely sorry for what he has done and for the publicity given to his case. I also talked to the doctor, and he says that his complete recovery is assured. Bobby is determined now to go back to school and get an education. In some ways, it is good that you and Lucy were abroad when this happened. By the time you get home, Bobby will be there. He has consented to stay with us until your arrival.

As you know, I got in touch with State, and it appears that they will take him come September. In the light of developments, I feel sure it is best that he drop out of Kingston and make a fresh start. In many ways there are added burdens to being the son of the Dean. Bobby is a good student and a grand boy; he'll come through with flying colors, never fear. Lucy must have been frantic, but tell her not to push the panic button. You still have two girls and another boy coming along!

You ask for advice in dealing with Bobby. If I have any suggestions, they would be: let out the line a bit, respect his individuality and private preferences; don't put him down, but build him up; regiment and control as little as possible. Let go of his hand, and above all, give freedom commensurate with responsibility.

Permit a little of the British to rub off on you. Live with the fog and keep a stiff upper lip!

Your friend,
Wesley